# 180 Days of READING
## for Prekindergarten

Darcy Mellinger, M.A.T., NBCT

**Consultant**

**Cathy Collier, M.S.Ed.**
Early Childhood Education Specialist

**Publishing Credits**

Corinne Burton, M.A.Ed., *Publisher*
Emily R. Smith, M.A.Ed., *VP of Content Development*
Andrew Greene, M.A.Ed., *Senior Content Manager*
Lynette Ordoñez, *Content Specialist*
Dani Neiley, *Associate Editor*
Jill Malcolm, *Multimedia Specialist*

**Standards**

© 2014 Mid-continent Research for Education and Learning
© Copyright 2007–2021 Texas Education Agency (TEA). All Rights Reserved.
© 2012 English–Language Arts Content Standards for California Public Schools by the California Department of Education.
© Copyright 2010 National Governors Association Center for Best Practices and Council of Chief State School Officers. All rights reserved.
© 2021 TESOL International Association
© 2021 Board of Regents of the University of Wisconsin System

**Image Credits:** p. 32 top right Andrew Greene; pp. 193, 201 Jill Malcolm; all other images from iStock and/or Shutterstock

A division of Teacher Created Materials
5482 Argosy Avenue
Huntington Beach, CA 92649-1039
**www.tcmpub.com/shell-education**
**ISBN 978-1-0876-5202-3**
© 2022 Shell Educational Publishing, Inc.

# Table of Contents

# What Do the Experts Say?

Welcome to *180 Days of Reading for Prekindergarten*! The most important concepts students will learn prior to entering kindergarten are practiced in the pages of this book. These practice pages can also be useful for students in kindergarten and first grade or older students who need extra support in learning the foundational skills of reading.

## Foundations

To prepare young learners for reading in kindergarten, practicing foundational skills will give them a great advantage. Repetition is a key to success for new readers. It is estimated that 85–90 percent of brain growth occurs in the first five years of life (First Things First 2017). In this book, students practice initial reading skills and combine them to begin understanding text on a page. The findings in the National Reading Panel's research document (2000) were instrumental in creating *180 Days of Reading for Prekindergarten*:

> It is essential to teach letters as well as phonemic awareness (PA) to beginners. PA training is more effective when children are taught to use letters to manipulate phonemes. This is because knowledge of letters is essential for transfer to reading and spelling. Learning all the letters of the alphabet is not easy, particularly for children who come to school knowing few of them. Shapes, names, and sounds need to be overlearned so that children can work with them automatically to read and spell words. Thus, if children do not know letters, this needs to be taught along with PA. (chap. 2, page 41)

Additionally, research has indicated that teaching phonics instruction earlier than first grade is more effective because it has the "biggest impact on growth in reading" (National Reading Panel 2000, chap. 2, page 93). By working through this book, children who are three to five years old and beginning to learn phonics and phonemic awareness will obtain the foundational reading skills to succeed in the elementary school setting.

# Repetition

A key to mastering high-frequency words is repetition, repetition, repetition! The 25 words practiced in the *High-Frequency Words* section of this book (pages 151–176) were selected from the beginning lists of words from Edward Fry's *1,000 Instant Words: The Most Common Words for Teaching Reading, Writing, and Spelling* (1999). Other high-frequency words are explored in different sections of this book as well. For example, the words *I* and *a* are practiced during the *Alphabet Practice* section.

In this book, students will practice these words with repetition. Several high-frequency words can be found in the *Segmenting Sounds* and *Reading Simple Words* sections of this book. Seeing these words multiple times is key to learning to recognize and read them, so students will see these words in print throughout the sections *Concepts of Print* and *Putting It All Together* as well.

# Practice Pages

The activities in this book will reinforce prekindergarten reading skills in a variety of ways. Each full page of practice is easy to prepare. You may use these pages to start the morning routine, launch the day's reading lesson, or provide follow-up lessons. Regardless of how the pages are used, students will be engaged in practicing the foundational skills to learn how to read through these standards-based activities.

# What Do the Experts Say? (cont.)

## Sequence of Learning

The order in which children learn reading basic skills is of the utmost importance. It is likened to the concept of scaffolding a building, where the foundation must be secure before building higher. The order of these skills was given great consideration during the creation of this resource. Be sure to follow the pages in the order they appear to gain the most from its contents.

In the first section of the book, students will learn to identify and write the consonant capital letters and connect their associated sounds. Next, students will learn to identify and write the lowercase consonants and connect their associated sounds. The order in which the letters are presented follows the sequence of the consonant letters in the research-based writing program Handwriting Without Tears (Olsen 2018). The organization is based on how the letters are formed. This allows students to more easily make connections among letters as they learn how to write them. Students will next learn the vowels, both capital and lowercase. They will practice long-vowel sounds first, followed by short-vowel sounds.

Once students have learned the alphabet, there is a section that introduces students to the nuances of the concepts of print. In the section that follows, students practice blending and segmenting sounds. The following section focuses on the ever-important high-frequency words, which are a key part of reading because students should know these words by sight recognition so that more effort can be given to other, newer words in sentences. Students then work through a section where they learn to read simple, three-letter words with short-vowel sounds as the middle sounds. This resource ends with a section called Putting It All Together in which students combine the skills previously learned so they can successfully start reading.

Finally, there are extra files to support students' learning in the Digital Resources as they conclude their exhilarating day-by-day journey of learning how to read.

# How to Use This Book

## "Introducing the Concept" Pages

To help teachers and parents/guardians understand each new section in *180 Days of Reading for Prekindergarten*, there will be an "Introducing the Concept" section. These pages will support adults to guide young learners through each topic.

Section overviews explain new concepts covered in the upcoming pages.

Materials lists provide suggestions that will help students as they complete the activities.

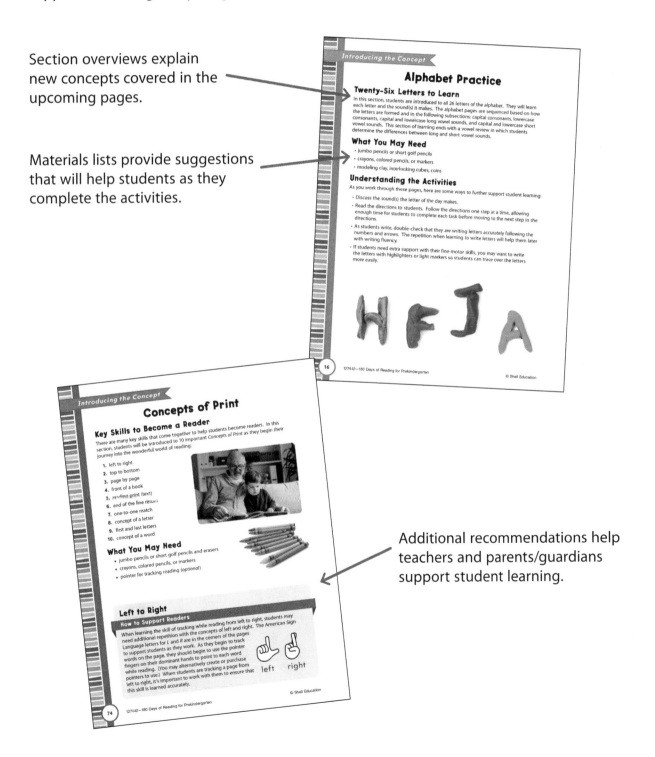

Additional recommendations help teachers and parents/guardians support student learning.

# How to Use This Book *(cont.)*

## Using the Practice Pages

The practice pages in this book provide instructional opportunities for each of the 180 days of the school year. Activities are organized into content themes. Teachers may plan to prepare packets of the practice pages for students. Each day's reading skill is aligned to reading standards that can be found on pages 14–15.

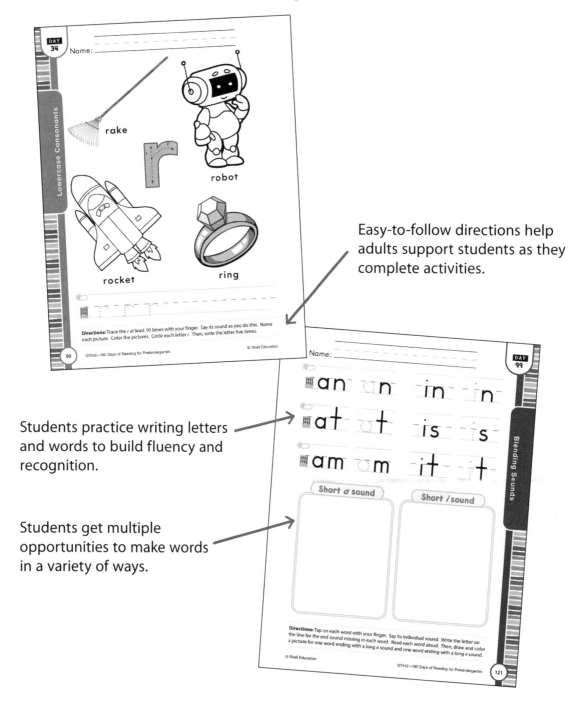

Easy-to-follow directions help adults support students as they complete activities.

Students practice writing letters and words to build fluency and recognition.

Students get multiple opportunities to make words in a variety of ways.

# Proper Pencil Grip

It is important for children to learn how to properly grip their pencils early. Students will naturally find their dominant hand. If a student writes with both their right and their left hand, brain research indicates that it is preferred to allow them to write with both hands. Younger students may have to grow into this grip, so encourage students to try this grip when you see that they are ready. The best pencil grip for children is with their pointer finger on the top, thumb on the side, and three fingers below the pencil to support the grip. The grip of the pencil is about one inch from the tip of the pencil. When students write throughout the pages of this book, encourage proper pencil grip.

Teach students to use sharpened pencils when it is time to write. Students will use their nondominant hands to hold down their papers or books. Posture is important, so invite students to sit tall with their backs supported by chairs. Their chairs should be a comfortable distance from the table where they are working. Teach students to press down on pencils with medium strength—not too hard and not too softly. Flexible seating is encouraged after proper grip and writing of letters has been mastered. To learn more about this topic, you can check out *How to Hold a Pencil* by Megan Hirsch (2010).

# Activities Overview

Over the upcoming 180 days of learning, students will begin to see language in new and exciting ways. Students will grow beautifully from newcomers to the alphabet to emerging readers who see words that surround their lives.

## Let's Learn Alphabet Letters

The letters of the alphabet are the foundation of reading, and these pages will allow students to interact with each letter. Students will practice the capital and lowercase alphabet, learn the difference between consonants and vowels, learn each alphabet sound, and write all alphabet letters accurately. Students will explore the following activities in this section.

| | |
|---|---|
| Scavenger Hunt | Give students the opportunity to look around to find objects that begin with the letter and sound of the day. This is an exciting way to practice the sound the letter makes and find objects with the same beginning sound. |
| Write Letters | During this activity, help students learn the sequence to properly write each letter on the line. Show them how to write letters on the line using the "sky, fence, and grass." |
| Make Letters with Your Body | After students investigate the letter of the day, have them make the letter with their bodies. They can either make it alone or recruit partners to make the shape of the letter of the day. |
| Use Objects | Help students use small objects to make the letter of the day in creative ways. Suggested nonchoking objects to use while supervising students include: modeling clay, interlocking cubes, coins, beans, etc. |

### Using the "Sky, Fence, and Grass" to Write

There are different ways to write letters. This book suggests forming letters using methods that generally do not require students to lift their pencils off the page. To support students in writing letters, this book has writing.

Use the sky, fence, and grass to help students understand how to use the writing lines: sky = top line, fence = midline, and grass = bottom line.

## You Can Explore a Book

In the *Concepts of Print* section, students learn how to maneuver through a book. They will practice how to follow text from left to right, top to bottom, and page by page. Then, they will learn how to identify the cover of a book. Students will learn that reading is a process. They will practice how to return to the following line at the end of a line of text. They will practice reading words with a one-to-one match by tracking the words with their pointer fingers. This section ends with students looking at the concepts of what a letter is, what a word is, and where the first and last letters are in a word. Practicing these concepts of print will support students as they move into other aspects of reading.

## What's That Sound?

Blending and segmenting sounds are the important next skills for emergent readers to practice. In the section *Blending Sounds*, students will learn to blend sounds together to read small, two-letter words and compound words. Blending sounds to read words involves seamlessly saying the sounds together to make a word. The section following blending sounds is *Segmenting Sounds*, where readers are encouraged to segment consonant-vowel-consonant (CVC) words. Segmenting words involves pulling a word apart to hear the separate sounds. These two sections allow students to write the blends and the segments. Practicing blending and segmenting sounds with use of oral language is a key way to support and extend the learning of these concepts.

# Activities Overview (cont.)

## Wonderful Words!

High-frequency words are those most often seen in print, such as *and*, *my*, *on*, *as*, *to*, *see*, *the*, *like*, and *play*. In this section, 25 words have been selected for reading practice. Students will learn the words and engage in activities to read them with automaticity upon sight. When students read high-frequency and simple words, they feel like detectives cracking a code. The more high-frequency words students know, the more successful they will be when reading sentences in text. The 25 words selected for this book are:

| up | if | her | the | you |
|----|----|-----|-----|-----|
| my | on | has | his | for |
| by | as | see | put | like |
| of | to | she | get | love |
| do | and | are | was | play |

## Review Pages

Throughout this book, students will have opportunities to periodically review alphabet letters and sounds. This review is emphasized in *180 Days of Reading for Prekindergarten* to support student retention of these key skills. Students will practice these concepts in the beginning of this book, so review and repetition are essential for maintaining these previously learned concepts. Identifying alphabet letters and knowing the sounds of each letter is fundamental to reading and will be important to review.

# Reading Simple Words

In this section of practice pages, students will learn to blend sounds together and begin reading simple words. The words in this section may be called consonant-vowel-consonant (CVC) words or word-family words. These simple words rhyme, such as *cat*, *bat*, *mat*, and *sat*. As students practice reading CVC words, they will begin to read them with automaticity. When students begin to read these words upon sight, it will help them become more fluent at reading print. As students grow by reading simple words along with high-frequency words, fluency will have a positive impact on their reading comprehension.

# Putting It All Together

Like an exclamation point at the end of a sentence, this *Putting It All Together* section is an exciting end to *180 Days of Reading for Prekindergarten*. This book is organized in a manner that scaffolds learning for students to prepare them to read. After practicing with the previous pages in this book, students will be putting together all the skills to read the words in print on these practice pages. Students will practice reading different fiction, nonfiction, and other forms of print found in the real world. It is a beautiful thing to behold when children begin to read. On the last day of practice (Day 180), you may use the certificate to celebrate students' learning achievements.

# Standards Correlations

Shell Education is committed to producing educational materials that are research and standards based. To support this effort, this resource is correlated to the academic standards of all 50 states, the District of Columbia, the Department of Defense Dependent Schools, and the Canadian provinces. A correlation is also provided for key professional educational organizations.

To print a customized correlation report for your state, please visit our website at **www.tcmpub.com/administrators/correlations** and follow the online directions. If you require assistance in printing correlation reports, please contact the Customer Service Department at 1-800-858-7339.

## College and Career Readiness Standards

The activities in this book are aligned to the following college and career readiness (CCR) standards:

| | |
|---|---|
| Alphabet Practice (days 1–57) | **Foundational Skills: Print Concepts**<br>• Recognize and name all upper and lowercase letters of the alphabet.<br>**Foundational Skills: Phonics and Word Recognition**<br>• Know and apply grade-level phonics and word-analysis skills in decoding words.<br>• Demonstrate basic knowledge of one-to-one letter-sound correspondences by producing the primary sound or many of the most frequent sounds for each consonant.<br>• Associate the long and short sounds with common spellings (graphemes) for the five major vowels.<br>**Foundational Skills: Phonological Awareness**<br>• Demonstrate understanding of spoken words, syllables, and sounds (phonemes). |
| Concepts of Print (days 58–97) | **Foundational Skills: Print Concepts**<br>• Demonstrate understanding of the organization and basic features of print.<br>• Follow words from left to right, top to bottom, and page by page.<br>• Recognize that spoken words are represented in written language by specific sequences of letters.<br>• Understand that words are separated by spaces in print.<br>**Informational Text: Key Ideas and Details**<br>• Identify the front cover of a book. |

| Blending and Segmenting Sounds (days 98–127) | **Foundational Skills: Phonological Awareness**<br>• Count, pronounce, blend, and segment syllables in spoken words.<br>• Blend and segment onsets and rimes of single-syllable spoken words. |
|---|---|
| High-Frequency Words (days 128–152) | **Foundational Skills: Phonics and Word Recognition**<br>• Know and apply grade-level phonics and word-analysis skills in decoding words.<br>• Read common high-frequency words by sight (e.g., *the, of, to, you, she, my, is, are, do, does*). |
| Reading Simple Words (days 153–162) | **Foundational Skills: Phonological Awareness**<br>• Recognize and produce rhyming words.<br>• Isolate and pronounce the initial, medial vowel, and final sounds (phonemes) in three-phoneme (consonant-vowel-consonant, or CVC) words.<br>• Add or substitute individual sounds (phonemes) in simple, one-syllable words to make new words. |
| Putting It All Together (days 163–180) | **Foundational Skills: Fluency**<br>• Read emergent-reader texts with purpose and understanding. |

# TESOL and WIDA Standards

In this book, the following English language development standards are met: Standard 1: English language learners communicate for social and instructional purposes within the school setting. Standard 2: English language learners communicate information, ideas, and concepts necessary for academic success in the content area of language arts.

# Alphabet Practice

## Twenty-Six Letters to Learn

In this section, students are introduced to all 26 letters of the alphabet.  They will learn each letter and the sound(s) it makes.  The alphabet pages are sequenced based on how the letters are formed and in the following subsections: capital consonants, lowercase consonants, capital and lowercase long-vowel sounds, and capital and lowercase short-vowel sounds.  This section of learning ends with a vowel review in which students determine the differences between long and short vowel sounds.

## What You May Need

- jumbo pencils or short golf pencils
- crayons, colored pencils, or markers
- modeling clay, interlocking cubes, coins
- small, nonchoking objects for letter-covering activities (modeling clay, interlocking cubes, beans, coins, etc.)

## Understanding the Activities

As you work through these pages, here are some ways to further support student learning:

- Discuss the sound(s) the letter of the day makes.
- Read the directions to students.  Follow the directions one step at a time, allowing enough time for students to complete each task before moving to the next step in the directions.
- As students write, double-check that they are writing letters accurately following the numbers and arrows.  The repetition when learning to write letters will help them later with writing fluency.
- If students need extra support with their fine-motor skills, you may want to write the letters with highlighters or light markers so students can trace the letters.

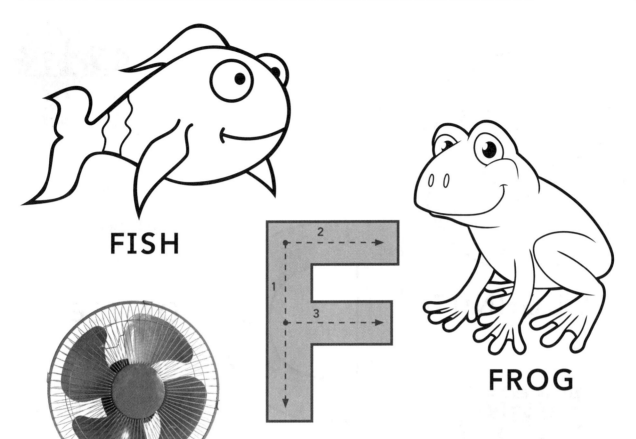

FISH

FAN

FROG

## Time to Draw

**Directions:** Trace the *F* at least 10 times with your finger. Say its sound as you do this. Name each picture. Color the pictures. Circle each letter *F*. Then, go on a scavenger hunt to find objects that begin with the *F* sound, and draw one of the objects.

Name: _____

**DOUGHNUT**

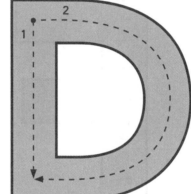

**DANCE**

**DOOR**

**DUCK**

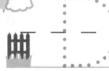

**Directions:** Trace the *D* at least 10 times with your finger. Say its sound as you do this. Name each picture. Color the pictures. Circle each letter *D*. Then, write the letter five times.

Name: _____

**PIG**

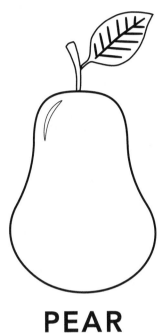

**PEAR**

**POPCORN**

**Time to Draw**

**Directions:** Trace the *P* at least 10 times with your finger. Say its sound as you do this. Name each picture. Color the pictures. Circle each letter *P*. Then, make the letter with your body, and draw how you did it.

Name: _____

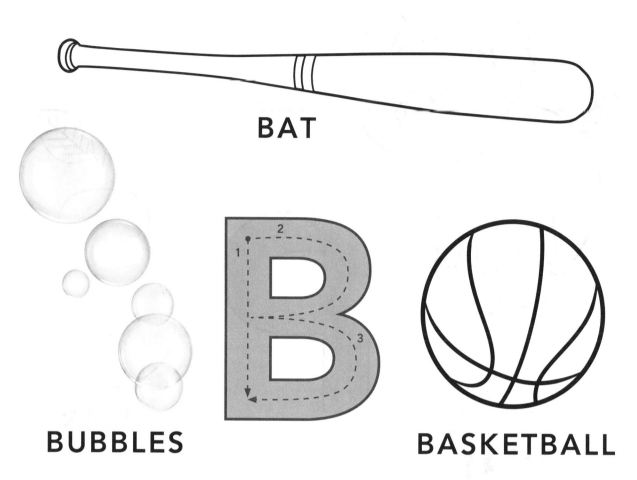

BAT

BUBBLES

BASKETBALL

BEAR

**Directions:** Trace the *B* at least 10 times with your finger. Say its sound as you do this. Name each picture. Color the pictures. Circle each letter *B*. Then, cover the letter with small objects.

Name: _____

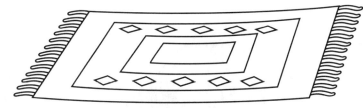

**RUG**

**READ**

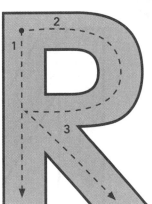

**RAINBOW**

**Time to Draw**

**Directions:** Trace the *R* at least 10 times with your finger. Say its sound as you do this. Name each picture. Color the pictures. Circle each letter *R*. Then, go on a scavenger hunt to find objects that begin with the *R* sound, and draw one of the objects.

Name: _____

Capital Consonants

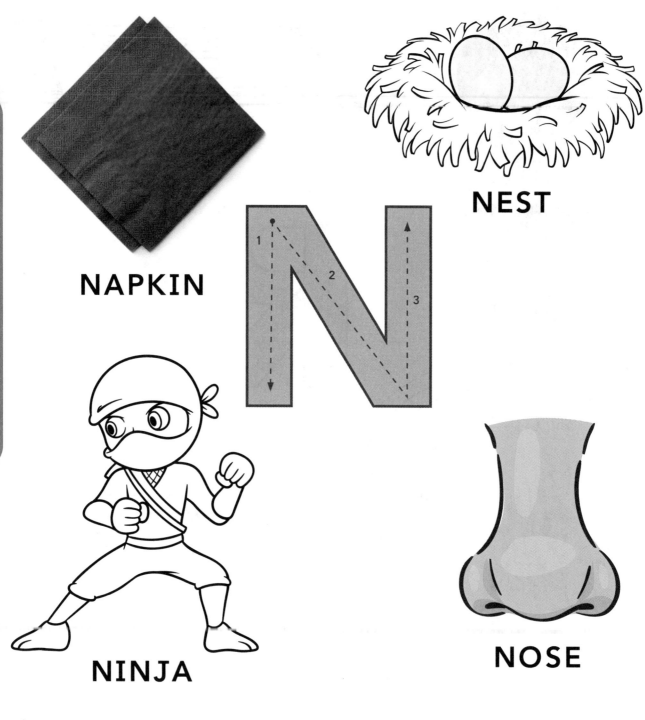

NAPKIN

NEST

NINJA

NOSE

**Directions:** Trace the *N* at least 10 times with your finger. Say its sound as you do this. Name each picture. Color the pictures. Circle each letter *N*. Then, write the letter five times.

MUSIC

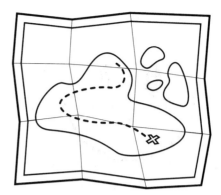

MAP

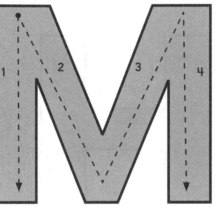

MILK

MONKEY

**Time to Draw**

**Directions:** Trace the *M* at least 10 times with your finger. Say its sound as you do this. Name each picture. Color the pictures. Circle each letter *M*. Then, make the letter with your body and a partner. Draw how you did it.

Name: _____

**Capital Consonants**

HAPPY

HAMMER

HOUSE

HAT

**Directions:** Trace the *H* at least 10 times with your finger. Say its sound as you do this. Name each picture. Color the pictures. Circle each letter *H*. Then, cover the letter with small objects.

Name: _____

KIWI

K

KITE

KOALAS

**Time to Draw**

**Directions:** Trace the *K* at least 10 times with your finger. Say its sound as you do this. Name each picture. Color the pictures. Circle each letter *K*. Then, go on a scavenger hunt to find objects that begin with the *K* sound, and draw one of the objects.

Name: _____

LADDER

LEAF

LOLLIPOP

LEMON

**Directions:** Trace the *L* at least 10 times with your finger. Say its sound as you do this. Name each picture. Color the pictures. Circle each letter *L*. Then, write the letter five times.

Name: _____

VOLLEYBALL

VAN

VOLCANO

**Time to Draw**

**Directions:** Trace the *V* at least 10 times with your finger. Say its sound as you do this. Name each picture. Color the pictures. Circle each letter *V*. Then, make the letter with your body, and draw how you made it.

Name: _____

**Capital Consonants**

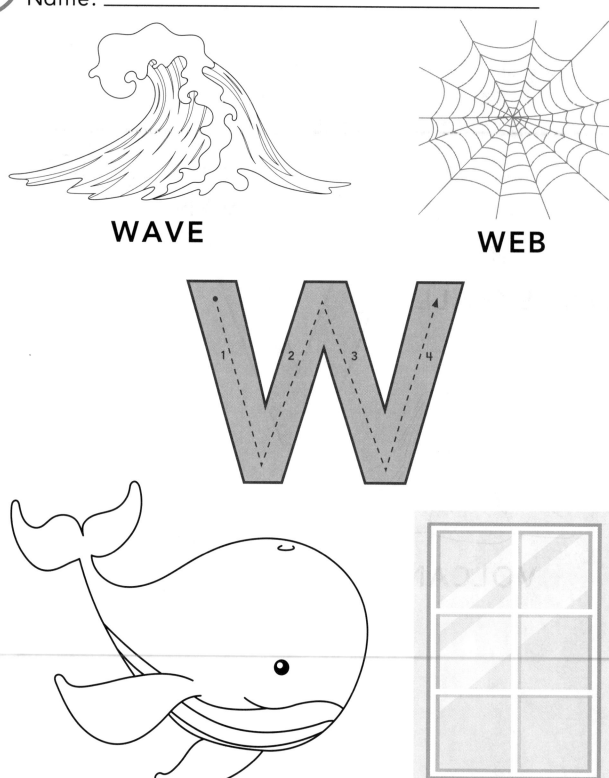

WAVE

WEB

WHALE

WINDOW

**Directions:** Trace the *W* at least 10 times with your finger. Say its sound as you do this. Name each picture. Color the pictures. Circle each letter *W*. Then, cover the letter with small objects.

Name: _____

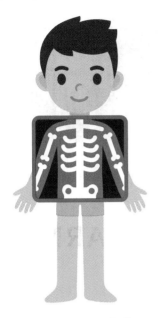

X-RAY

OX

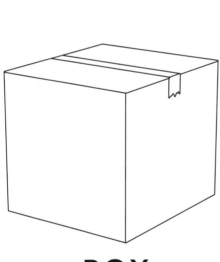

BOX

**Time to Draw**

**Directions:** Trace the *X* at least 10 times with your finger. Say its sound as you do this. Name each picture. Color the pictures. Circle each letter *X*. Then, make the letter with your body, and draw how you made it.

Name: _____

Capital Consonants

YO-YO

YARN

YOGURT

YAK

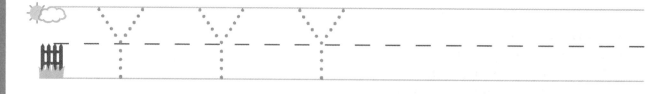

**Directions:** Trace the *Y* at least 10 times with your finger. Say its sound as you do this. Name each picture. Color the pictures. Circle each letter *Y*. Then, write the letter five times.

Name: _____

**ZEBRA**

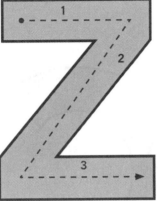

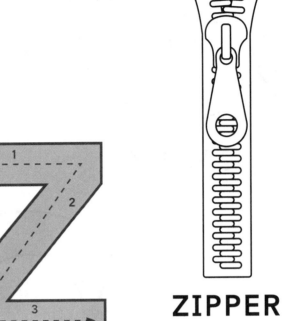

**ZIPPER**

**ZOO**

**Time to Draw**

**Directions:** Trace the *Z* at least 10 times with your finger. Say its sound as you do this. Name each picture. Color the pictures. Circle each letter *Z*. Then, make the letter with your body, and draw how you made it.

Name: _____

CANDY

CAT

C

COCONUT

CARD

**Directions:** Trace the C at least 10 times with your finger. Say its sound as you do this. Name each picture. Color the pictures. Circle each letter C. Then, cover the letter with small objects.

Name: _____

QUEEN

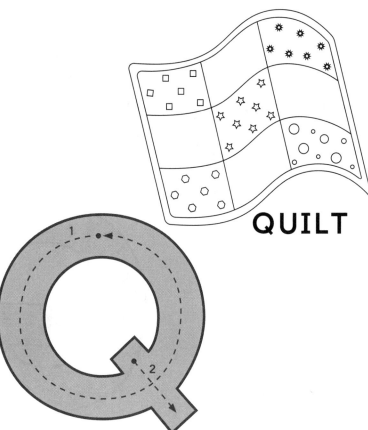

QUILT

QUARTER

**Time to Draw**

**Directions:** Trace the *Q* at least 10 times with your finger. Say its sound as you do this. Name each picture. Color the pictures. Circle each letter *Q*. Then, make the letter *Q* with small objects. Draw what you made.

Name: _____

GUM

GRAPES

GORILLA

GRASS

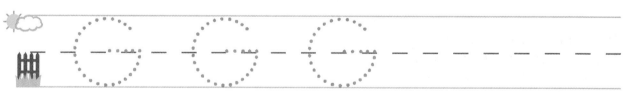

**Directions:** Trace the *G* at least 10 times with your finger. Say its sound as you do this. Name each picture. Color the pictures. Circle each letter *G*. Then, write the letter five times.

Name: _____

SMILE

SUN

STRAWBERRY

**Time to Draw**

**Directions:** Trace the *S* at least 10 times with your finger. Say its sound as you do this. Name each picture. Color the pictures. Circle each letter *S*. Then, make the letter with your body, and draw how you made it.

**TURTLE**

**TOMATO**

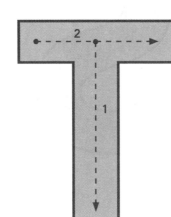

**TEDDY BEAR**

**TACO**

**Directions:** Trace the *T* at least 10 times with your finger. Say its sound as you do this. Name each picture. Color the pictures. Circle each letter *T*. Then, cover the letter with small objects.

Name: _____

JUMP

JELLYFISH

JAM

**Time to Draw**

**Directions:** Trace the *J* at least 10 times with your finger. Say its sound as you do this. Name each picture. Color the pictures. Circle each letter *J*. Then, go on a scavenger hunt to find objects that begin with the *J* sound, and draw one of the objects.

Name: _____

Lowercase Consonants

carrots

cap

cupcake

corn

**Directions:** Trace the c at least 10 times with your finger. Say its sound as you do this. Name each picture. Color the pictures. Circle each letter c. Then, write the letter five times.

Name: _____

sleep

sandwich

S

seal

**Time to Draw**

**Directions:** Trace the *s* at least 10 times with your finger. Say its sound as you do this. Name each picture. Color the pictures. Circle each letter *s*. Then, go on a scavenger hunt to find objects that begin with the *S* sound, and draw one of the objects.

Name: _____

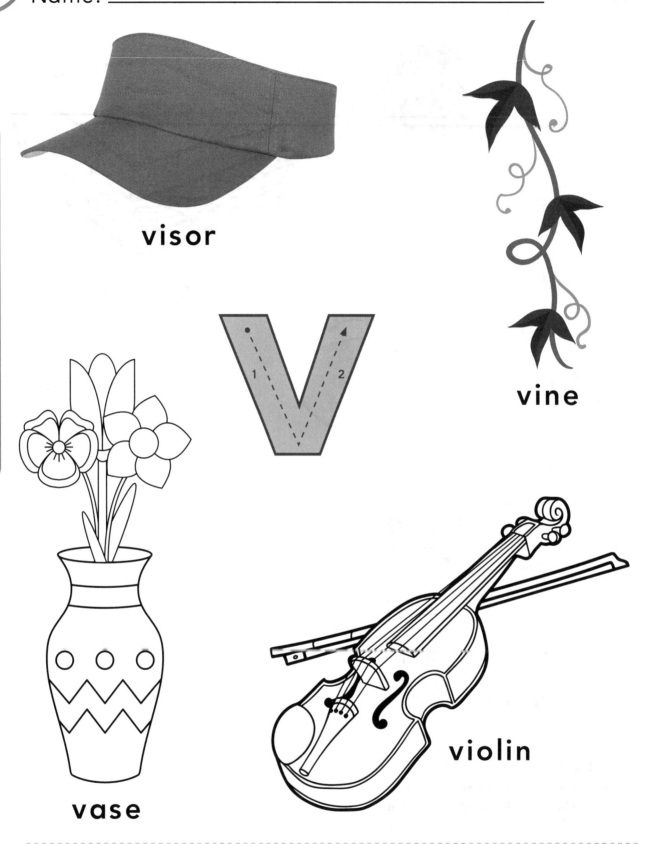

visor

vine

vase

violin

**Directions:** Trace the *v* at least 10 times with your finger. Say its sound as you do this. Name each picture. Color the pictures. Circle each letter *v*. Then, cover the letter with small objects.

Name: _____

water

walk

worm

**Time to Draw**

**Directions:** Trace the *w* at least 10 times with your finger. Say its sound as you do this. Name each picture. Color the pictures. Circle each letter *w*. Then, go on a scavenger hunt to find objects that begin with the *w* sound, and draw one of the objects.

Name: _____

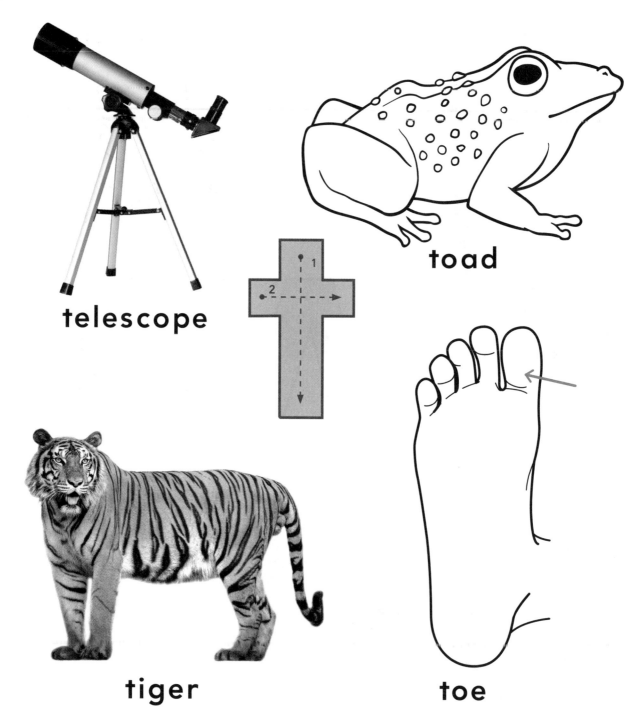

telescope

toad

tiger

toe

---

**Directions:** Trace the *t* at least 10 times with your finger. Say its sound as you do this. Name each picture. Color the pictures. Circle each letter *t*. Then, write the letter five times.

Name: _____

doctor

dog

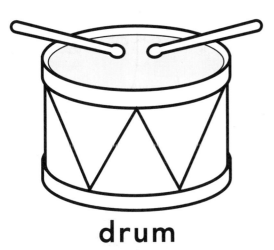

drum

**Time to Draw**

**Directions:** Trace the *d* at least 10 times with your finger. Say its sound as you do this. Name each picture. Color the pictures. Circle each letter *d*. Then, make the letter with your body, and draw how you made it.

Name: _____

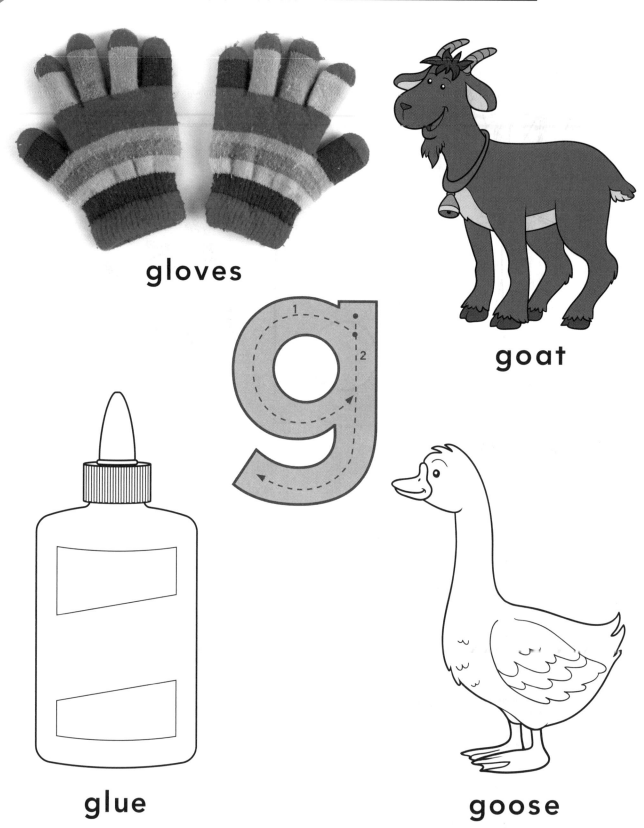

gloves

goat

glue

goose

**Directions:** Trace the *g* at least 10 times with your finger. Say its sound as you do this. Name each picture. Color the pictures. Circle each letter *g*. Then, cover the letter with small objects.

lake

leg

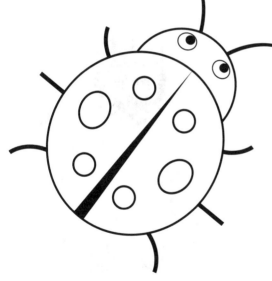

ladybug

**Time to Draw**

**Directions:** Trace the *l* at least 10 times with your finger. Say its sound as you do this. Name each picture. Color the pictures. Circle each letter *l*. Then, go on a scavenger hunt to find objects that begin with the *l* sound, and draw one of the objects.

Name: _____

key

kitten

kangaroo

king

**Directions:** Trace the *k* at least 10 times with your finger. Say its sound as you do this. Name each picture. Color the pictures. Circle each letter *k*. Then, write the letter five times.

Name: _____

yam

yell

y

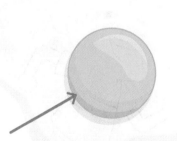

yolk

**Time to Draw**

**Directions:** Trace the *y* at least 10 times with your finger. Say its sound as you do this. Name each picture. Color the pictures. Circle each letter *y*. Then, make the letter with your body, and draw how you made it.

Name: _____

Lowercase Consonants

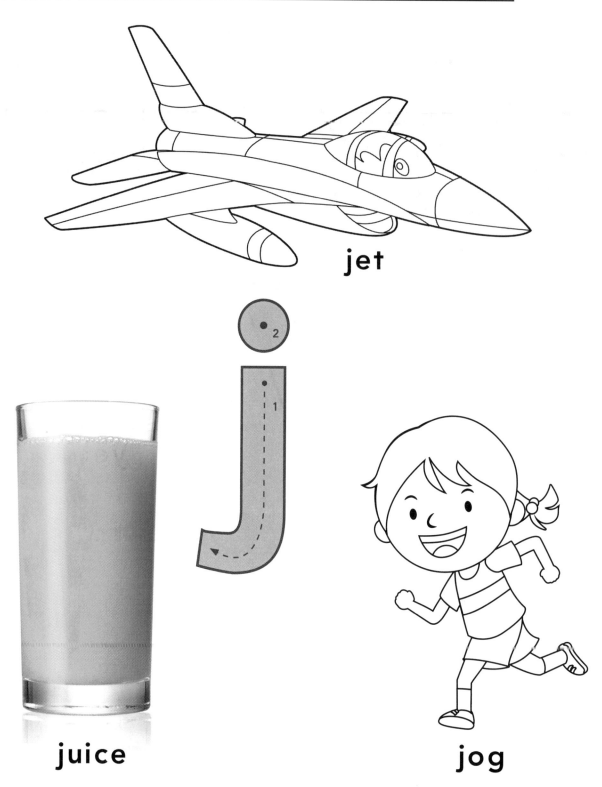

jet

juice

jog

**Directions:** Trace the *j* at least 10 times with your finger. Say its sound as you do this. Name each picture. Color the pictures. Circle each letter *j*. Then, cover the letter with small objects.

Name: _____

pumpkin

peanut

pizza

**Time to Draw**

**Directions:** Trace the *p* at least 10 times with your finger. Say its sound as you do this. Name each picture. Color the pictures. Circle each letter *p*. Then, go on a scavenger hunt to find objects that begin with the *p* sound, and draw one of the objects.

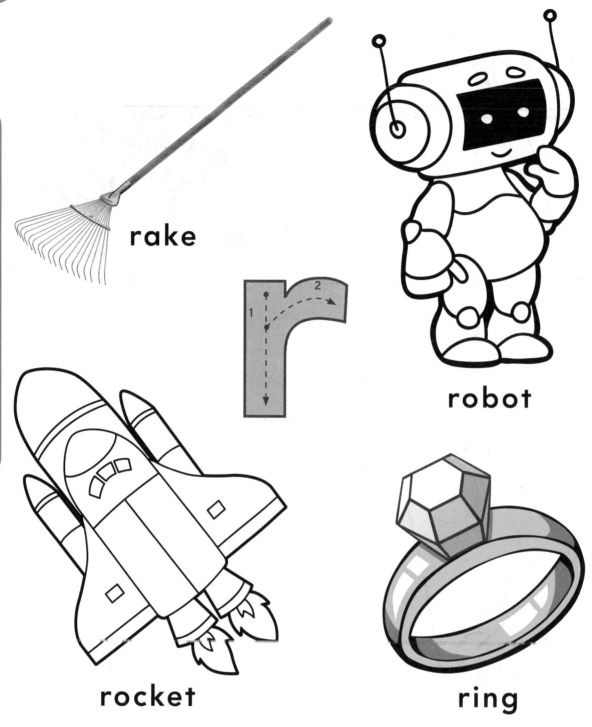

rake

robot

rocket

ring

**Directions:** Trace the *r* at least 10 times with your finger. Say its sound as you do this. Name each picture. Color the pictures. Circle each letter *r*. Then, write the letter five times.

Name: _____

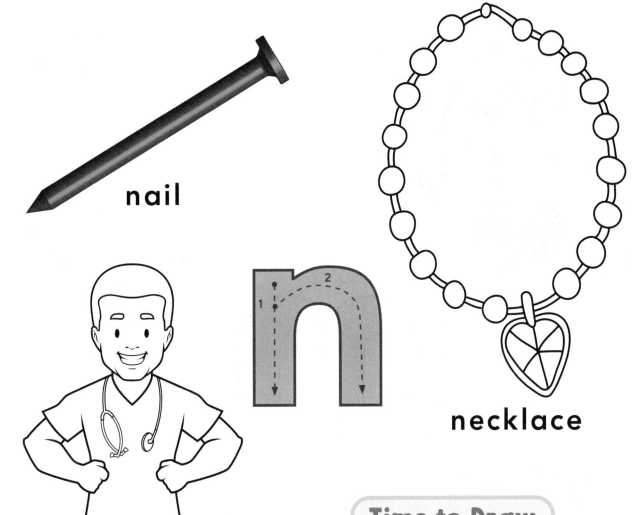

nail

necklace

n

nurse

**Time to Draw**

**Directions:** Trace the *n* at least 10 times with your finger. Say its sound as you do this. Name each picture. Color the pictures. Circle each letter *n*. Then, make the letter with your body, and draw how you made it.

Lowercase Consonants

mug

moon

mouse

mountain

**Directions:** Trace the *m* at least 10 times with your finger. Say its sound as you do this. Name each picture. Color the pictures. Circle each letter *m*. Then, cover the letter with small objects.

Name: _____

horse

heart

hippo

**Time to Draw**

**Directions:** Trace the *h* at least 10 times with your finger. Say its sound as you do this. Name each picture. Color the pictures. Circle each letter *h*. Then, go on a scavenger hunt to find objects that begin with the *h* sound, and draw one of the objects.

Name: _____

book

broccoli

bus

banana

**Directions:** Trace the *b* at least 10 times with your finger.  Say its sound as you do this.  Name each picture.  Color the pictures.  Circle each letter *b*.  Then, write the letter five times.

Lowercase Consonants

Name: _____

feet

fox

fork

**Time to Draw**

**Directions:** Trace the *f* at least 10 times with your finger. Say its sound as you do this. Name each picture. Color the pictures. Circle each letter *f*. Then, make the letter with your body, and draw how you made it.

Name: _____

question

quail

quiet

quack

**Directions:** Trace the *q* at least 10 times with your finger. Say its sound as you do this. Name each picture. Color the pictures. Circle each letter *q*. Then, cover the letter with small objects.

Name: _____

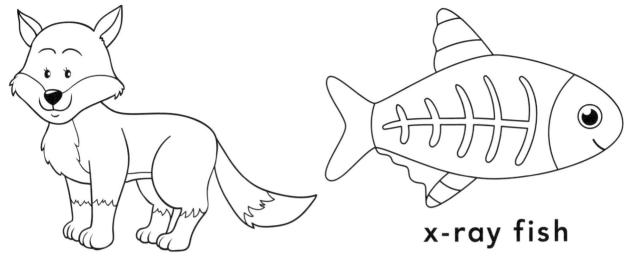

fox

x-ray fish

six

**Time to Draw**

**Directions:** Trace the *x* at least 10 times with your finger. Say its sound as you do this. Name each picture. Color the pictures. Circle each letter *x*. Then, make the letter *x* with clay or small objects. Draw what you made.

Name: _____

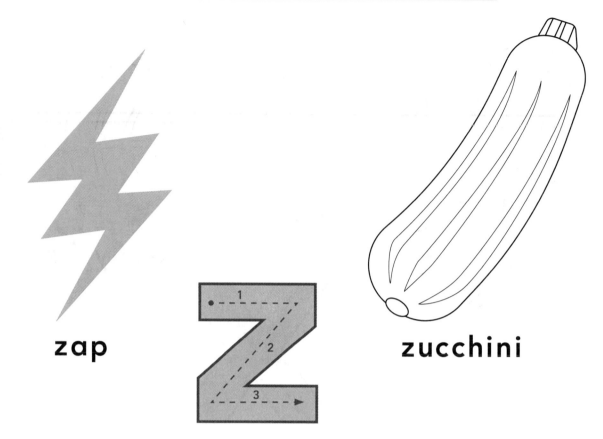

**zap**

**zucchini**

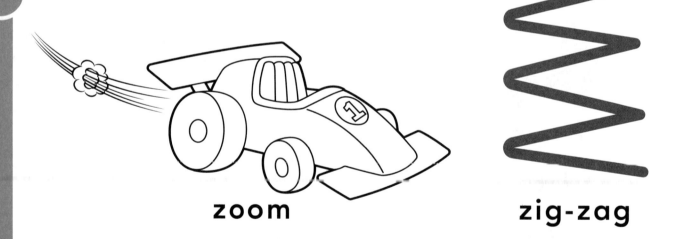

**zoom**

**zig-zag**

**Directions:** Trace the *z* at least 10 times with your finger. Say its sound as you do this. Name each picture. Color the pictures. Circle each letter *z*. Then, write the letter five times.

**APE**

**APRON**

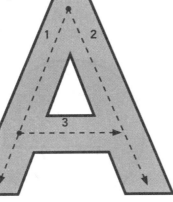

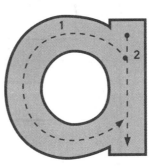

**acorn**

**Time to Draw**

**Directions:** Trace the *A* and *a* letters at least 10 times with your finger. Say the long *a* sound as you do this. Name each picture. Color the pictures. Circle each letter *A* and each letter *a*. Then, make the capital and lowercase letters with your body and a partner. Draw how you made them.

Long Vowels

Name: _____

eat

eagle

EASEL

EEL

**Directions:** Trace the *E* and *e* letters at least 10 times with your finger. Say the long *e* sound as you do this. Name each picture. Color the picture. Circle each letter *E* and each letter *e*. Then, cover the large *E* and *e* letters with small objects.

© Shell Education

Name: _____

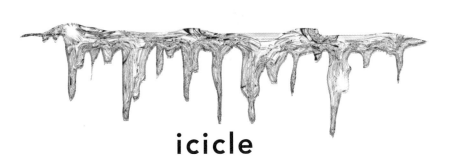

icicle

ICE CREAM

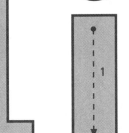

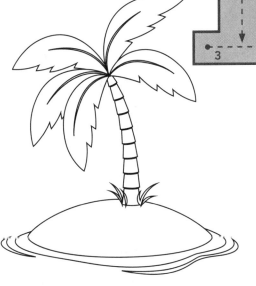

island

**Time to Draw**

**Directions:** Trace the *I* and *i* letters at least 10 times with your finger. Say the long *i* sound as you do this. Name each picture. Color the pictures. Circle each letter *I* and each letter *i*. Then, make the capital and lowercase letters with your body, and draw how you made them.

**Long Vowels**

Name: _____

**OCEAN**

**oatmeal**

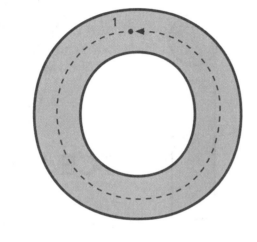

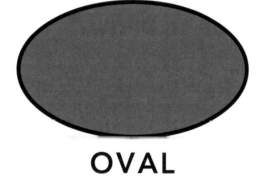

**OVAL**

**overalls**

**Directions:** Trace the *O* and *o* letters at least 10 times with your finger. Say the long *o* sound as you do this. Name each picture. Color the pictures. Circle each letter *O* and each letter *o*. Then, write the letters three times.

uniform

UNICORN

UTENSILS

**Time to Draw**

**Directions:** Trace the *U* and *u* letters at least 10 times with your finger. Say the long *u* sound as you do this. Name each picture. Color the pictures. Circle each letter *U* and each letter *u*. Then, make the capital and lowercase letters with your body, and draw how you made them.

Name: _____

APPLE

astronaut

ANT

acrobat

**Directions:** Trace the *A* and *a* letters at least 10 times with your finger. Say the short *a* sound as you do this. Name each picture. Color the pictures. Circle each letter *A* and each letter *a*. Then, cover the large *A* and *a* letters with small objects.

Short Vowels

egg

ELEPHANT

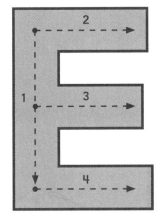

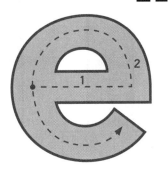

exercise

Time to Draw

**Directions:** Trace the *E* and *e* letters at least 10 times with your finger. Say the short *e* sound as you do this. Name each picture. Color the pictures. Circle each letter *E* and each letter *e*. Then, make the capital and lowercase letters with your body and a partner. Draw how you made them.

Name: _____

IGLOO

insect

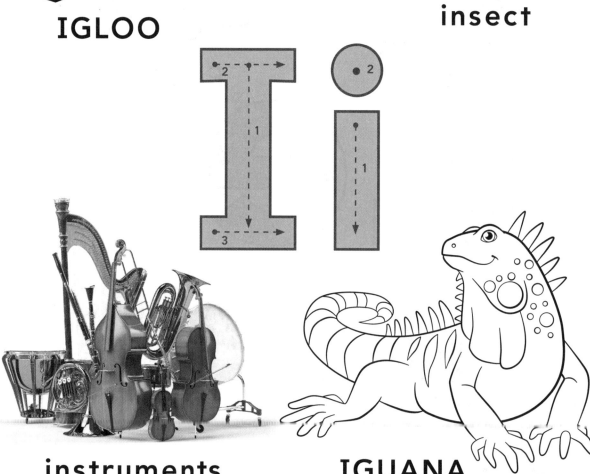

instruments

IGUANA

**Directions:** Trace the *I* and *i* letters at least 10 times with your finger. Say the short *i* sound as you do this. Name each picture. Color the pictures. Circle each letter *I* and each letter *i*. Then, write the letters four times.

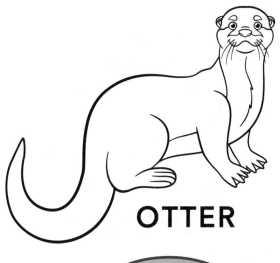

**OTTER**

**OCTOPUS**

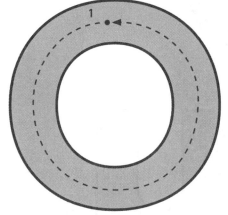

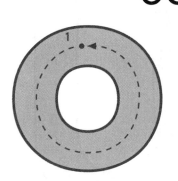

**OX**

## Time to Draw

**Directions:** Trace the *O* and *o* letters at least 10 times with your finger. Say the short *o* sound as you do this. Name each picture. Color the pictures. Circle each letter *O* and each letter *o*. Then, make the capital and lowercase letters with your body, and draw how you made them.

Name: _____

UMPIRE

umbrella

UP

unhappy

**Directions:** Trace the *U* and *u* letters at least 10 times with your finger. Say the short *u* sound as you do this. Name each picture. Color the pictures. Circle each letter *U* and each letter *u*. Then, cover the large *U* and *u* letters with small objects.

apron

antelope

ate

acrobat

## Time to Draw

| Word Beginning with Long *a* Sound | Word Beginning with Short *a* Sound |
|---|---|
| | |

**Directions:** Trace the *A* and *a* letters at least 10 times with your finger. Say the short and long vowel sounds as you do this. Name each picture. Draw and color a picture of another word that begins with a long *a* sound and another word that begins with a short *a* sound.

Name: _____

Vowels Review

equal

elf

elevator

eat

## Time to Draw

| Word Beginning with Long *e* Sound | Word Beginning with Short *e* Sound |
|---|---|
|  |  |

**Directions:** Trace the *E* and *e* letters at least 10 times with your finger. Say the short and long vowel sounds as you do this. Name each picture. Draw and color a picture of another word that begins with a long *e* sound and another word that begins with a short *e* sound.

idea

inch

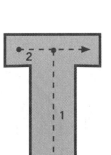

infant

ice

## Time to Draw

| Word Beginning with Long *i* Sound | Word Beginning with Short *i* Sound |
|---|---|
|  |  |

**Directions:** Trace the *I* and *i* letters at least 10 times with your finger. Say the short and long vowel sounds as you do this. Name each picture. Draw and color a picture of another word that begins with a long *i* sound and another word that begins with a short *i* sound.

**Vowels Review**

Name: _____

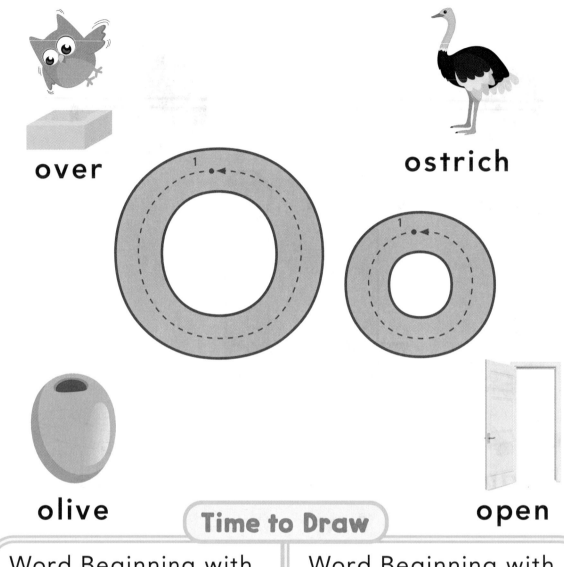

over

ostrich

olive

open

**Time to Draw**

| Word Beginning with Long *o* Sound | Word Beginning with Short *o* Sound |
|---|---|
| | |

**Directions:** Trace the *O* and *o* letters at least 10 times with your finger. Say the short and long vowel sounds as you do this. Name each picture. Draw and color a picture of another word that begins with a long *o* sound and another word that begins with a short *o* sound.

127442—180 Days of Reading for Prekindergarten

**unicycle**

**uphill**

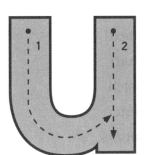

**umbrella**

**unicorn**

## Time to Draw

| Word Beginning with Long *u* Sound | Word Beginning with Short *u* Sound |
|---|---|
| | |

**Directions:** Trace the *U* and *u* letters at least 10 times with your finger. Say the short and long vowel sounds as you do this. Name each picture. Draw and color a picture of another word that begins with a long *u* sound and another word that begins with a short *u* sound.

# Concepts of Print

## Key Skills to Become a Reader

There are many key skills that come together to help students become readers. In this section, students will be introduced to 10 important concepts of print as they begin their journey into the wonderful world of reading:

1. left to right
2. top to bottom
3. page by page
4. front of a book
5. reading print (text)
6. end-of-line return
7. one-to-one match
8. concept of a letter
9. first and last letters
10. concept of a word

## What You May Need

- jumbo pencils or short golf pencils and erasers
- crayons, colored pencils, or markers
- pointer for tracking reading (*optional*)

## Left to Right

### How to Support Readers

When learning the skill of tracking while reading from left to right, students may need additional repetition with the concepts of left and right. The American Sign Language letters for *L* and *R* are in the corners of the pages to support students as they work. As they begin to track words on the page, they should begin to use the pointer fingers on their dominant hands to point to each word while reading. (You may alternatively create or purchase pointers to use.) When students are tracking a page from left to right, it's important to work with them to ensure that this skill is learned accurately.

left     right

# Top to Bottom

## How to Support Readers

When learning the skill of tracking while reading from the top to the bottom of a page, students will continue to track the words on the page from left to right, using the pointer fingers on their dominant hands or pointers. Work with students to combine these skills accurately by continuing to track left to right while reading from top to bottom of pages. Remember, these are new skills for emerging readers and sometimes it's easy to forget that everyone had to learn all these concepts at some point!

# Page by Page

## How to Support Readers

When learning the skill of tracking while reading from page to page, students will continue to track the words on the page from left to right and top to bottom, using the pointer fingers on their dominant hands or pointers. For the portion of the directions where they are learning to navigate from page to page, it's important to work with students to ensure that this skill is learned accurately. An extension of this skill is to use books in your library and make sure to turn only one page at a time, being gentle with the pages. This skill can also be practiced by turning the pages in this workbook each day going forward.

# Concepts of Print *(cont.)*

## Front of a Book

### How to Support Readers

Students will now learn how to find the front of the book, which is also called the *front cover*. Let's compare it to a cozy bed that has many layers of sheets and blankets with a cover on top. Similarly, the pages of a book are neatly tucked inside the book with its front cover on top. Discuss with students how the front cover of a book can help a reader decide whether they want to read that book. For example, if something on the cover is off-putting to a student, they might choose another book that looks more appealing to them. Reading the titles on front covers will be a new skill also. To extend students' understanding of the concept of the front cover, you may introduce the concepts of author and illustrator because this information will be found on the front covers of books. In this section, students will practice reading titles from left to right with their pointer fingers or pointers.

## Reading Print (Text)

### How to Support Readers

Students will investigate the difference between looking at and understanding the pictures on a page versus reading the text. Young readers infer information from pictures, and this is an important part of comprehension. The next step for students that now know letters, sounds, and words is to understand that reading involves *print*, or text. You can now explore the differences between the pictures and the print (or text) on the pages in books.

## End-of-Line Return

### How to Support Readers

**Let Freedom Ring**

The Liberty Bell rang when the Declaration of Independence was first read out loud.

In this section, students will focus on what to do at the end of a line of text. Previously, students learned to read from the top to the bottom, and this section focuses on the ends of the lines. Discuss with students that the end of the line and the path you take from one line to the next is where the reader's eyes should travel on the page. It is like a map that readers "travel" with their eyes. For a visual example, you can use a text application on your computer or cell phone for students to see how the cursor moves down at the end of a line. As students continue to track the words on the page, they will use pointers to move down at the end of each line.

# One-to-One Match

## How to Support Readers

It's time to get those pointer fingers or pointers ready to practice tracking individual words on the page! This involves matching spoken words to the words on the page, and it is a fabulous time to observe how students are doing with tracking while exploring the concepts of print. It will be helpful to read the sentences with students to see how the one-to-one match while tracking is coming along. Once you have read it together once or twice, students can practice independently. An extension of learning for this concept might be having students track with pointers while you read the cover of a magazine, the title of an internet article, or any phrase or sentence you might see in print. Students can always use their pointer fingers to track while you read so they can show you how they can apply the one-to-one match while reading.

# Concept of a Letter

## How to Support Readers

In this section, students will learn about the concept of a letter. First, they will review the concept of a letter within a word, and then they will look at the concept of a letter within print. It is time to apply what students have already learned about the letters of the alphabet to text on book pages. This is also a great time to reinforce the letters and their sounds. A method of extending students' learning of this concept is to begin "reading" the world where students live. Begin to read print together everywhere! Words surround students and can be found in advertisements, street signs, food wrappers, billboards, toy packaging, magazine covers, commercials, etc. When you see words in the real world, ask students to tell you one letter within each word. Watch students enjoy letters!

I can

read words!

# Concepts of Print (cont.)

## First and Last Letters

### How to Support Readers

Now that students are familiar with the concept of a letter within print, it's time to get a little more specific and help them learn about the first and last letters of a word. Once students review that skill, they can apply it to finding the first and last letters of words within text. Continue to extend students' learning in their daily lives. You may want to take pictures of interesting letters and words you find and even make a book of those pictures. Make sure to talk with students about the first and last letters within the words you see.

## Concept of a Word

### How to Support Readers

It is an exciting time for students to show what is understood about the concept of a word within text. This is the culmination of understanding letter sounds, matching spoken words to text, and realizing that words are separated by spaces on the page. Reading the pages together with students helps them to see all the concepts of print merge together. One way to continue exploring the concept of a word with students is to start a list or a collection of favorite words students may see or hear. This can be a group project for children and adults alike.

Name: _____

I   can   run   fast.

1   2   3   4

→   →   →   →

I   can   blow   this   bubble.

1   2   3   4   5

→   →   →   →   →

**Time to Draw**

**Directions:** Tap on each word with your finger. Move your finger from the left side of the sentence to the right side. Circle each letter *i*. Then, draw something you can do.

Left to Right

I     have     this     lollipop.

1 →   2 →     3 →     4 →

We     have     a     happy     family.

1 →    2 →     3 →   4 →       5 →

**Time to Draw**

**Directions:** Tap on each word with your finger. Move your finger from the left side of the sentence to the right side. Circle each letter *a*. Then, draw something you have.

Name: _____

Left to Right

We    will    sleep.

1 →    2 →    3 →

I    will    read.

1 →    2 →    3 →

**Time to Draw**

**Directions:** Tap on each word with your finger. Move your finger from the left side of the sentence to the right side. Circle each letter *e*. Then, draw something you will do.

Name: _____

**Top to Bottom**

I   am   happy   to   swing.
1   2   3   4   5
→   →   →   →   →

I   can   fly   like   a   bird.
1   2   3   4   5   6
→   →   →   →   →   →

I   am   feeding   my   dog.
1   2   3   4   5
→   →   →   →   →

He   really   loves   to   eat.
1   2   3   4   5
→   →   →   →   →

**Directions:** Tap on each word with your finger. Move your finger from the left side of the sentence to the right side *and* from the top to the bottom of the page. Circle each word *am*. Act out different things you may do to finish this sentence: *I am….*

Name: _____

I play with my best friend.
1 → 2 → 3 → 4 → 5 → 6 →

We like to play fun games.
1 → 2 → 3 → 4 → 5 → 6 →

It is fun to play.
1 → 2 → 3 → 4 → 5 →

**Time to Draw**

**Directions:** Tap on each word with your finger. Move your finger from the left side of the sentence to the right side *and* from the top to the bottom of the page. Circle each word *play*. Draw your favorite game.

Name: _____

I go out for ice cream.
1  2  3  4  5  6
→ → → → → →

I get my favorite flavor.
1  2  3  4  5
→ → → → →

We swim in the lake.
1  2  3  4  5
→ → → → →

The water is warm to us.
1  2  3  4  5  6
→ → → → → →

**Directions:** Tap on each word with your finger. Move your finger from the left side of the sentence to the right side *and* from the top to the bottom of the page. Circle the letters *l* and *i*. Act out the sentences.

**64**

**Directions:** Tap on each word with your finger. Move your finger from the left side of the sentence to the right side, from the top to the bottom of the page, and page by page. Circle each word *has*. Then, act out one of these pages.

127442—180 Days of Reading for Prekindergarten

Page by Page

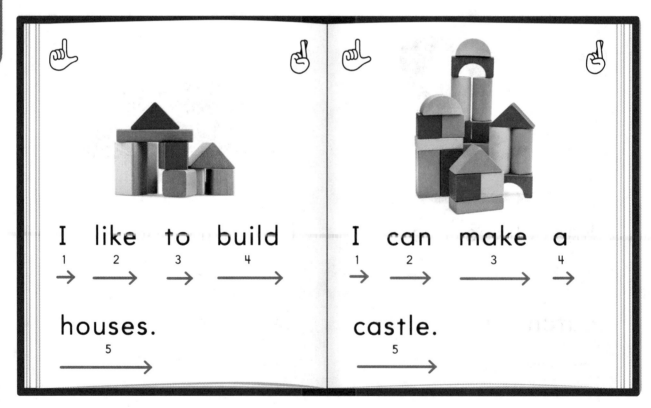

**Directions:** Tap on each word with your finger. Move your finger from the left side of the sentence to the right side, from the top to the bottom of the page, and page by page. Circle each word *like*. Find a book in your home to gently turn from page to page.

He has a new
1    2    3    4
→    →    →    →

puppy.
5
→

The puppy likes
1      2      3
→      →      →

to walk.
4    5
→    →

The puppy has
1     2     3
→     →     →

a bone.
4   5
→   →

The puppy can
1     2     3
→     →     →

run with it.
4    5    6
→    →    →

**Directions:** Tap on each word with your finger. Move your finger from the left side of the sentence to the right side, from the top to the bottom of the page, and page by page. Circle each word *has*. Then, act out one of these pages.

Name: _____

Front of a Book

They are in 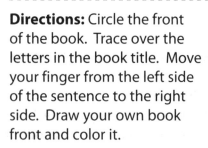.

leaves

6

**Time to Draw**

**Directions:** Circle the front of the book. Trace over the letters in the book title. Move your finger from the left side of the sentence to the right side. Draw your own book front and color it.

Name: _____

A map shows a **place**.

4

## Time to Draw

**Directions:** Circle the front of the book. Trace over the letters in the book title. Move your finger from the left side of the sentence to the right side. Draw and color the front of a book you would like to write.

Name: _____

**Front of a Book**

# Come Home, Cats

**Dona Herweck Rice**

The 🐱🐱🐱 were
cats

in the 🌿.
grass

10

## Time to Draw

**Directions:** Circle the front of the book. Trace over the letters in the book title. Move your finger from the left side of the sentence to the right side, and from the top to the bottom of the page. Draw and color the front of a book you would write about your favorite animal.

Name: _____

These are my friends.

2

3

We like each other.

4

5

**Directions:** Circle the text on each book page above. Tap on each word with your finger. Move your finger from the left side of the sentence to the right side on each page. Find print in other books.

Reading Print (Text)

Name: _____

I help with the cape.

2

I help with the hat.

3

**Time to Draw**

**Directions:** Circle the text on each book page above. Tap on each word with your finger. Move your finger from the left side of the sentence to the right side on each page. Draw how you help.

Name: _____

Big Ben has circles.

6

There are circles on the clock.

7

Big Ben has squares.

8

There are squares around the clock.

9

**Directions:** Circle the text on each book page above. Tap on each word with your finger. Move your finger from the left side of the sentence to the right side, and move it from the top to the bottom of the pages. Find circles and squares in your home.

**Name:** _____

Best, Best Day

This is when Grandpa gave me his goggles.

18

The next day, Boris walked to Pooch Park. Polly was waiting.

16

## Time to Draw

**Directions:** Find the text on each book page above. Tap on each word with your finger. Move your finger from the left side of the sentence to the right side, and move it from the top to the bottom of the page. Trace the path that you take with your eyes when you read the end of each line. Then, draw an animal that moves like that path.

Name: _____

Big Ben has shapes.

What shapes do you see?

14

15

## Time to Draw

**Directions:** Find the text on each book page above. Tap on each word with your finger. Move your finger from the left side of the sentence to the right side, and move it from the top to the bottom of the page. Trace the path that you take with your eyes when you read the end of each line. Then, draw and color the shapes you see.

Name: _____

**End-of-Line Return**

## Time to Draw

**Directions:** Find the text on each book page above. Tap on each word with your finger. Move your finger from the left side of the sentence to the right side, and move it from the top to the bottom of the page. Trace the path that you take with your eyes when you read the end of each line. Then, draw a vehicle that moves like that path.

Name: _____

This is a
→ pet hamster.

She likes to
→ hold it.

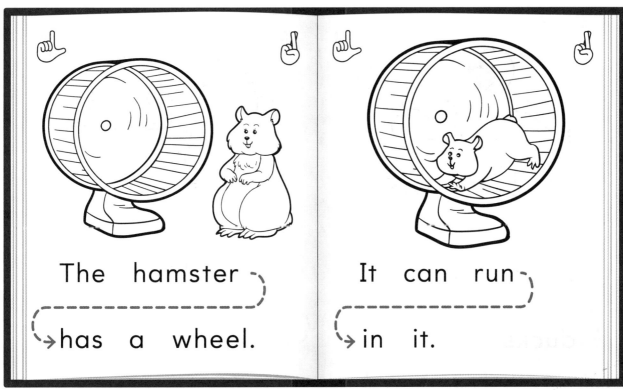

The hamster
→ has a wheel.

It can run
→ in it.

**Directions:** Tap on each word with your finger. Move your finger from the left side of the sentence to the right side, from the top to the bottom of the page, and page by page from left to right. Then, color the pictures.

Name: _____

We live by
a park.

It is nice to
play there.

I see the
ducks.

They like to
swim.

**Directions:** Tap on each word with your finger. Move your finger from the left side of the sentence to the right side, from the top to the bottom of the page, and page by page from left to right. Then, color the pictures.

One-to-One Match

Dad made a
nice meal.

My family sat
at the table.

The meal was
yummy.

I ate all
of it!

**Directions:** Tap on each word with your finger. Move your finger from the left side of the sentence to the right side, from the top to the bottom of the page, and page by page from left to right. Then, color the pictures.

Concept of a Letter

Name: _____

dog

cat

bird

bear

mouse

**Time to Draw**

**Directions:** Color the pictures. Circle only one letter in each word. Draw an animal. Write the word on the line to label your picture. Then, circle one letter in the word.

Name: _____

apple

grapes

orange

banana

strawberry

Time to Draw

**Directions:** Color the pictures. Circle only one letter in each word. Draw your favorite fruit. Write the word on the line to label your picture. Then, circle one letter in the word.

**Concept of a Letter**

Name: _____

We saw a rainbow.
It was very big!

**Time to Draw**

**Directions:** Circle only one letter in each word. Draw your favorite kind of weather. Label your picture. Then, circle one letter in the word.

Name: _____

doll

magnet

blocks

car

train

**Time to Draw**

---

**Directions:** Color the pictures. Circle the first letter in each word. Then, circle the last letter in each word. Draw how you like to play. Label your picture. Then, circle the first and last letters in the word.

---

Name: _____

First and Last Letters

jump

dance

run

skip

crawl

## Time to Draw

**Directions:** Color the pictures. Circle the first letter in each word. Then, circle the last letter in each word. Draw how you move your body. Label your picture. Then, circle the first and last letters in the word.

Name: _____

We heard music playing.
It was our time to dance!

**Time to Draw**

**Directions:** Circle the first letter in each word. Then, circle the last letter in each word. Draw how you feel about music or dancing. Label your picture. Then, circle the first and last letters in the word.

Name: _____

I used my pencil and markers.
The picture I made was beautiful!

**Time to Draw**

**Directions:** Circle five words. Tap on each word with your finger. Move your finger from left to right, top to bottom, and to show a return at the end of the line. Go on a word scavenger hunt in your home. Draw and color what you find.

Name: _____

I was happy for my special day.
My friends came to my birthday!

## Time to Draw

**Directions:** Circle five words. Tap on each word with your finger. Move your finger from left to right, top to bottom, and to show a return at the end of the line. Draw what makes you happy. Label your picture.

Name: _____

I played catch today.
I kept trying my best!

**Time to Draw**

**Directions:** Circle the first letter in each word. Then, circle the last letter in each word. Draw what you like to play with your friends. Label your picture. Then, circle the first and last letters in the word.

Name: _____

alphabet

friends

buttons

dig

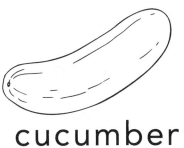

cucumber

**Time to Draw**

My Friends

---

**Directions:** Name each picture. Color the pictures. Circle the consonants *b*, *c*, *d*, and *f*. Draw you with your friends.

Letters and Sounds Review

Name: _____

goat

lamb

horse

invitation

kettle

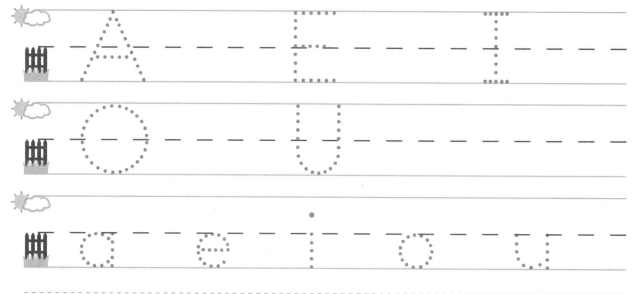

A        E        I

O        U

a    e    i    o    u

**Directions:** Name each picture.  Color the pictures.  Circle each vowel (*a, e, i, o, u*) in each word.  Trace and write the vowels.

Name: _____

necktie

potato

rice

money

queen

## Time to Draw

My Favorite Word

**Directions:** Name each picture. Color the pictures. Circle the consonants *m, n, p, q,* and *r*. Draw a picture to show your favorite word on this page.

Name: _____

sail

taste

x-ray

vine

wiggle

## Time to Draw

Food I Like to Taste

**Directions:** Name each picture. Color the pictures. Circle the consonants *s*, *t*, *v*, *w*, and *x*. Draw a food you like to taste.

Name: _____

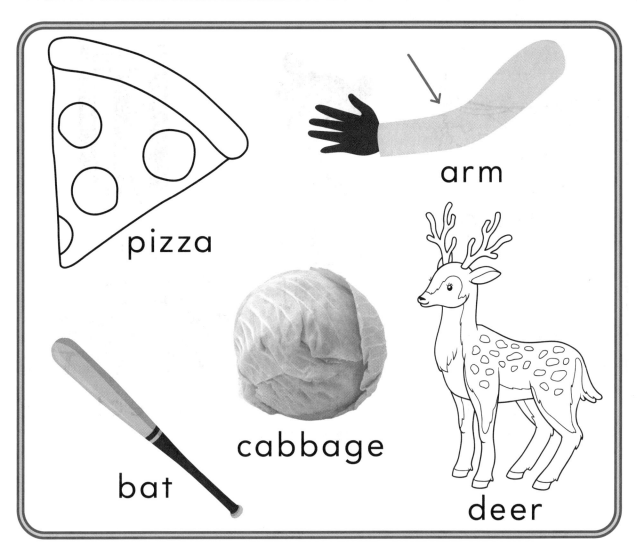

pizza

arm

bat

cabbage

deer

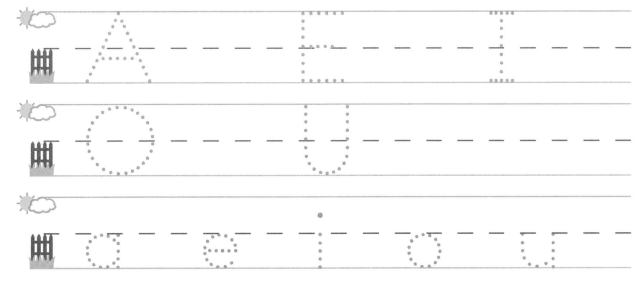

**Directions:** Name each picture. Color the pictures. Circle each vowel (*a, e, i, o, u*) in each word. Trace and write the vowels.

Name: _____

Letters and Sounds Review

hamburger

golf

jelly

frosting

insect

## Time to Draw

**Directions:** Name each picture. Color the pictures. Circle the consonants *f*, *g*, *h*, and *j*. Draw a picture to show your favorite word on this page.

Name: _____

lettuce

pony

mouse

kick

net

## Time to Draw

**Directions:** Name each picture. Color the pictures. Circle the consonants *k*, *l*, *m*, *n*, and *p*. Draw a mouse in its house.

Name: _____

**Letters and Sounds Review**

quiz

railroad

seeds

unicorn

tangerine

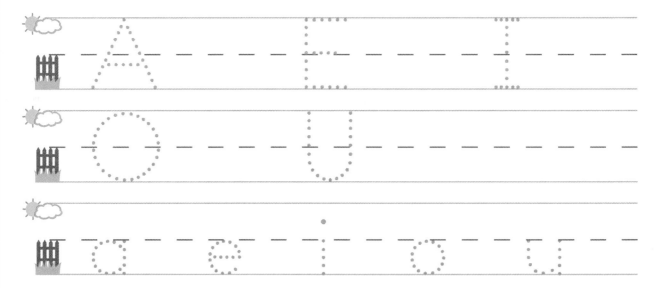

**Directions:** Name each picture. Color the pictures. Circle each vowel (*a, e, i, o, u*) in each word. Trace and write the vowels.

Name: _____

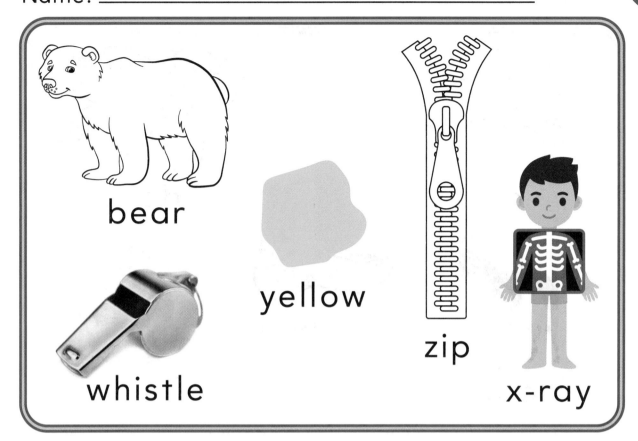

bear

yellow

whistle

zip

x-ray

## Time to Draw

**Directions:** Name each picture. Color the pictures. Circle the consonants *b*, *w*, *x*, *y*, and *z*. Draw a picture to show your favorite word on this page.

Name: _____

Letters and Sounds Review

cars

dolls

goat

heel

flames

Time to Draw

**Directions:** Name each picture. Color the pictures. Circle the consonants *c*, *d*, *f*, *g*, and *h*. Draw toys you like to play with, such as cars or dolls.

# Blending Sounds

## Learning to Read!

Students now know the letters of the alphabet, the sounds they make, and the essential concepts of print. It is time for students to take the individual sounds of letters and blend them together.

## What You May Need

- jumbo pencils with erasers or short golf pencils
- crayons, colored pencils, or markers
- pointer for tracking reading (*optional*)
- camera (*optional*)

## Understanding the Activities

Blending sounds is an exhilarating step in the journey of learning to read. As much as possible, engage with students in this pivotal phase as a guide to model blending sounds to make words. Gradually release ownership to students when you observe them blending independently.

Name: _____

**Blending Sounds**

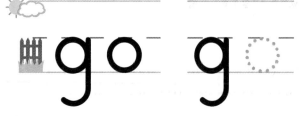

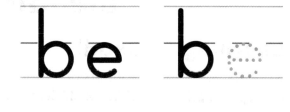

**Long *o* Sound**

**Long *e* Sound**

**Directions:** Tap on each word with your finger. Say its individual sound. Write the letter on the line for the ending sound missing in each word. Read each word aloud. Then, draw a picture to show one word ending with a long *o* sound and one word ending with a long *e* sound.

127442—180 Days of Reading for Prekindergarten

© Shell Education

Name: _____

| Short *a* Sound | Short *i* Sound |
| --- | --- |
| | |

**Directions:** Tap on each word with your finger. Say its individual sound. Write the letter on the line for the beginning sound missing in each word. Read each word aloud. Then, draw a picture to show one word beginning with a short *a* sound and one word beginning with a short *i* sound.

Blending Sounds

 hen  hen

 pen  p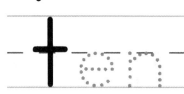en

ten  ten  10

## Short *e* Sound

**Directions:** Tap on each word with your finger. Say its individual sounds. Write the letters on the line for the ending sounds missing in each word. Read each word aloud. Then, draw a picture to show a word with a short *e* sound.

Name: _____

cat    c a t

rat    r a t

bat    b a t

## Short *a* Sound

**Directions:** Tap on each word with your finger. Say its individual sounds. Write the letters on the line for the ending sounds missing in each word. Read each word aloud. Then, draw a picture to show a word with a short *a* sound.

Name: _____

## Blending Sounds

rain•bow

rainbow

cup•cake

cupcake

**Time to Draw**

**Directions:** Trace each letter in the words with your finger. With an adult, say each part of the compound word. Then, blend the two parts together to say the word aloud. Write the compound words on the lines. Draw a picture to show one of the compound words.

Name: _____

cow•boy

star•fish

**Time to Draw**

**Directions:** Trace each letter in the words with your finger. With an adult, say each part of the compound word. Then, blend the two parts together to say the word aloud. Write the compound words on the lines. Draw a picture to show one of these words.

Name: _____

# fish•bowl

fishbowl

# fire•truck

fire•truck

## Time to Draw

**Directions:** Trace each letter in the words with your finger. With an adult, say each part of the compound word. Then, blend the two parts together to say the word aloud. Write the compound words on the lines. Draw a picture to show a new word. Write your word.

Name: _____

## tooth•brush

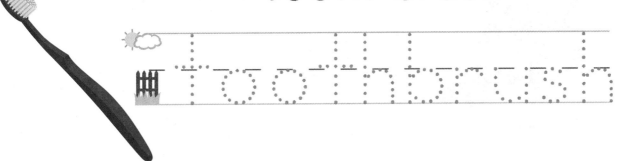

## rain•drop

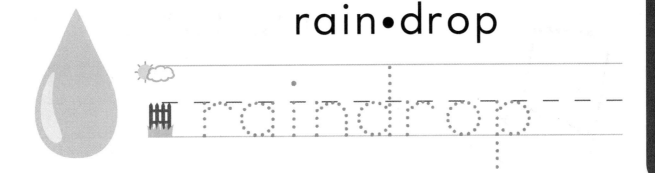

## Time to Draw

**Directions:** Trace each letter in the words with your finger. With an adult, say each part of the compound word. Then, blend the two parts together to say the word aloud. Write the compound words on the lines. Draw a picture to show the compound word that has the most letters. Write the word that has the most letters.

Name: _____

# mail•box

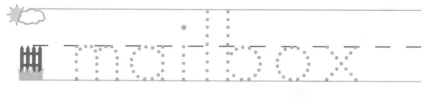

# lap•top

**Blending Sounds**

## Time to Draw

**Directions:** Trace each letter in the words with your finger. With an adult, say each part of the compound word. Then, blend the two parts together to say the word aloud. Write the compound words on the lines. Draw a picture to show one of these words.

snow•man

pop•corn

Time to Draw

**Directions:** Trace each letter in the words with your finger. With an adult, say each part of the compound word. Then, blend the two parts together to say the word aloud. Write the compound words on the lines. Draw a picture to show a new compound word. Write your word.

# Segmenting Sounds

## Learning to Read!

Students have learned many foundational skills of reading. Now, it is time to segment sounds. Students will practice saying and writing the letter sounds in words.

## What You May Need

- jumbo pencils with erasers or short golf pencils
- crayons, colored pencils or markers
- small, nonchoking objects for activities (modeling clay, interlocking cubes, beans, coins, etc.)
- pointer for tracking reading (*optional*)
- camera (*optional*)

## Understanding the Activities

Segmenting sounds is another exciting step in learning to read. Again, you are encouraged to engage with students as much as possible to model segmenting the sounds within a word, watching for their readiness to segment as independent readers.

Name: _____

**c + a + t = cat**

**j + a + m = jam**

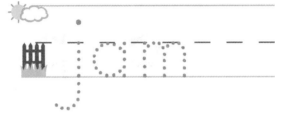

**m + a + t = mat**

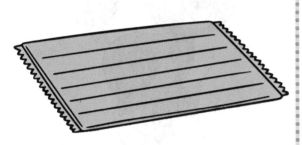

**h + a + t = hat**

**Directions:** Trace each letter in the word with your finger. Say each sound. Then, blend the three sounds together to say the word aloud. Write each word.

Name: _____

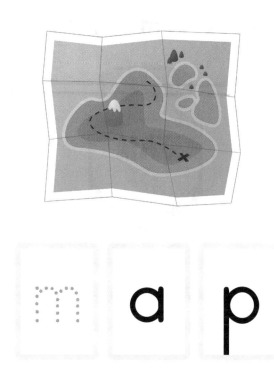

m a p

r a n

r a t

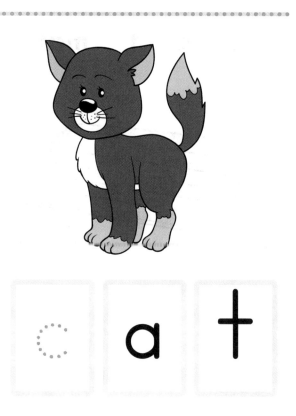

c a t

**Directions:** Write the missing letter for each word. Trace each letter in the word with your finger, and say each sound. Then, blend the three sounds together to say the word aloud. Make these words using small objects.

| w | e | t |
|---|---|---|

| n | e | t |
|---|---|---|

| b | e | d |
|---|---|---|

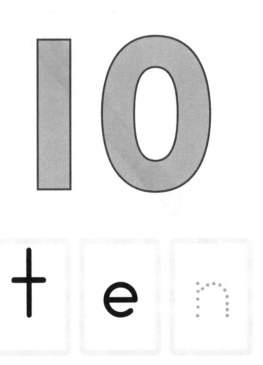

| t | e | n |
|---|---|---|

**Directions:** Write the missing letter for each word. Trace each letter in the word with your finger, and say each sound. Then, blend the three sounds together to say the word aloud. Make these words using small objects. Say words that rhyme with these words.

Name: _____

**Segmenting Sounds**

**j + e + t = jet**

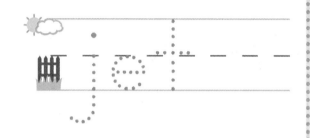

**r + e + d = red**

**p + e + n = pen**

**h + e + n = hen**

**Directions:** Trace each letter in the word with your finger. Say each sound. Then, blend the three sounds together to say the word aloud. Write each word.

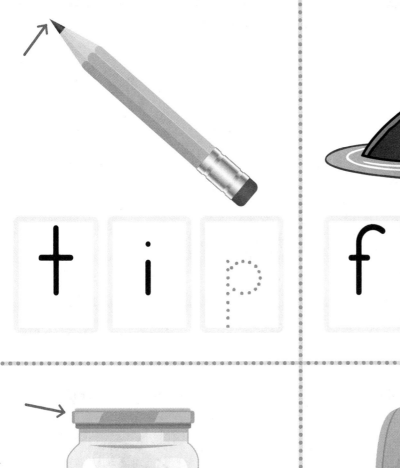

t i p

f i n

l i d

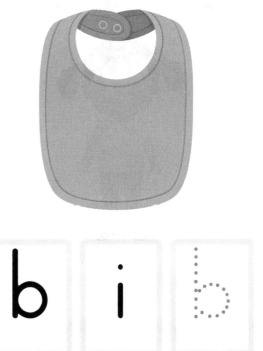

b i b

**Directions:** Write the missing letter for each word. Trace each letter in the word with your finger, and say each sound. Then, blend the three sounds together to say the word aloud. Make these words using small objects. Say words that rhyme with these words.

Name: _____

**Segmenting Sounds**

**d + i + p = dip**

**l + i + p = lip**

**k + i + d = kid**

**s + i + p = sip**

**Directions:** Trace each letter in the word with your finger. Say each sound. Then, blend the three sounds together to say the word aloud. Write each word.

c   o   t

b   o   x

h   o   t

m   o   p

**Directions:** Write the missing letter for each word. Trace each letter in the word with your finger, and say each sound. Then, blend the three sounds together to say the word aloud. Make these words using small objects.

d o g

h o p

p o p

t o p

**Directions:** Write the missing letter for each word. Trace each letter in the word with your finger, and say each sound. Then, blend the three sounds together to say the word aloud. Make these words using small objects. Say words that rhyme with these words.

Name: _____

Segmenting Sounds

**c + u + t = cut**

**h + u + g = hug**

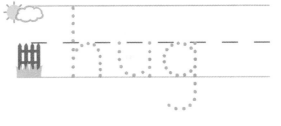

**n + u + t = nut**

**r + u + g = rug**

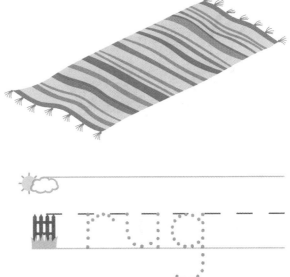

---

**Directions:** Trace each letter in the word with your finger. Say each sound. Then, blend the three sounds together to say the word aloud. Write each word.

---

Name: _____

Segmenting Sounds

t u b

p u p

b u g

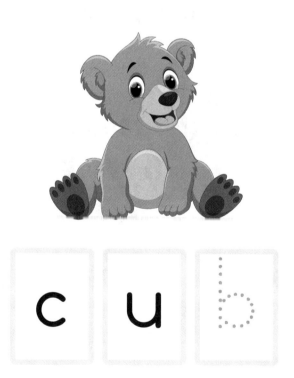

c u b

**Directions:** Write the missing letter for each word. Trace each letter in the word with your finger, and say each sound. Then, blend the three sounds together to say the word aloud. Make these words using small objects. Say words that rhyme with these words.

Name: _____

bed

cab

dips

fans

chocolate

**Time to Draw**

**Directions:** Name each picture. Color the pictures. Circle the consonants *b*, *c*, *d*, and *f*. Draw yourself with one of these words.

Letters and Sounds Review

Name: _____

umbrella

kickball

ill

jacks

licorice

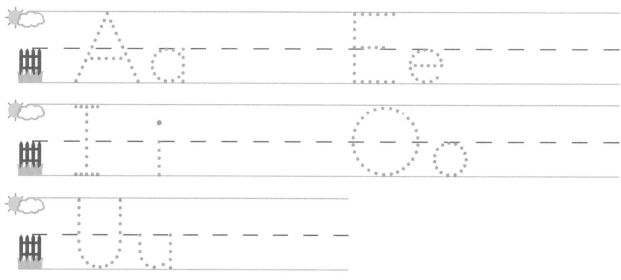

Aa    Ee

Ii    Oo

Uu

**Directions:** Name each picture. Color the pictures. Circle each vowel (*a, e, i, o, u*) in each word. Trace and write the vowels.

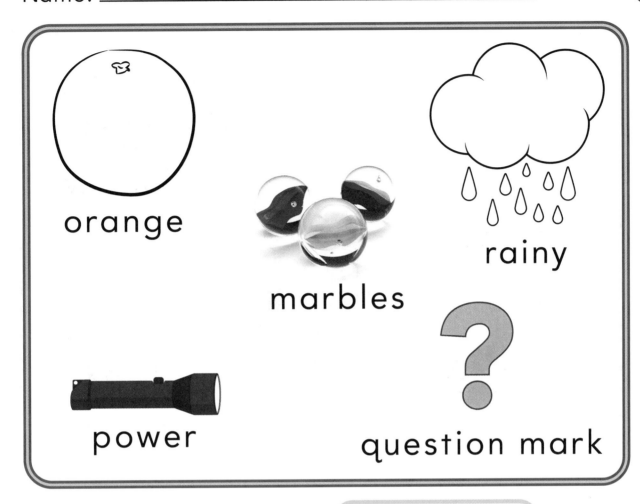

orange

marbles

rainy

power

question mark

## Time to Draw

**Directions:** Name each picture. Color the pictures. Circle the consonants *m*, *n*, *p*, *q*, and *r*. Draw your favorite word on this page.

Name: _____

Letters and Sounds Review

trees

xylophone

us

violets

world

## Time to Draw

**Directions:** Name each picture. Color the pictures. Circle the consonants *s*, *t*, *v*, *w*, and *x*. Draw yourself with one of these words.

Name: _____

zebra

cookies

young

bathtub

a

a

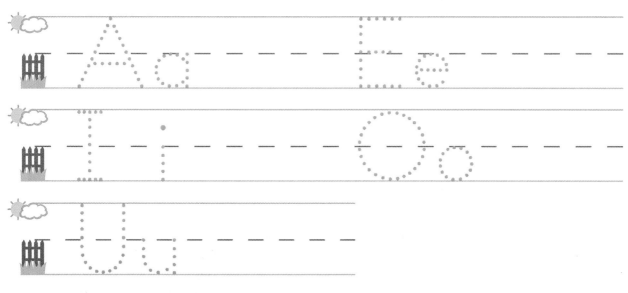

**Directions:** Name each picture.  Color the pictures.  Circle each vowel (*a, e, i, o, u*) in each word.  Trace and write the vowels.

Name: _____

Earth

friend

jay

guacamole

hen

## Time to Draw

**Directions:** Name each picture. Color the pictures. Circle the consonants *f*, *g*, *h*, and *j*. Draw your favorite word on this page.

Name: _____

ketchup

love

mustard

orangutan

notes

**Time to Draw**

**Directions:** Name each picture. Color the pictures. Circle the consonants *k*, *l*, *m*, *n*, and *p*. Draw yourself with one of these words.

Letters and Sounds Review

Name: _____

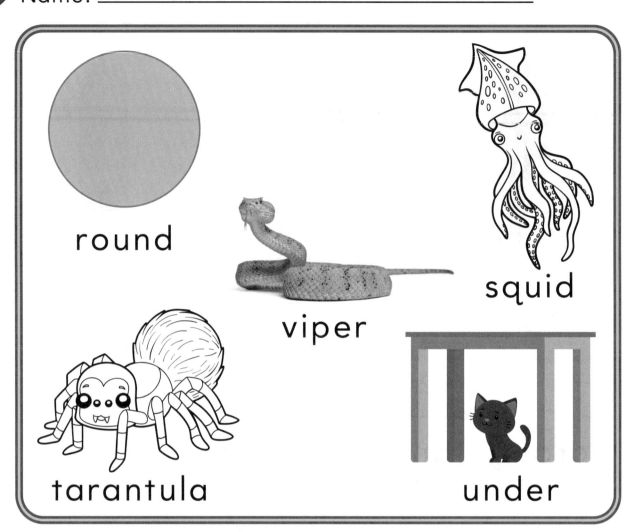

round

viper

squid

tarantula

under

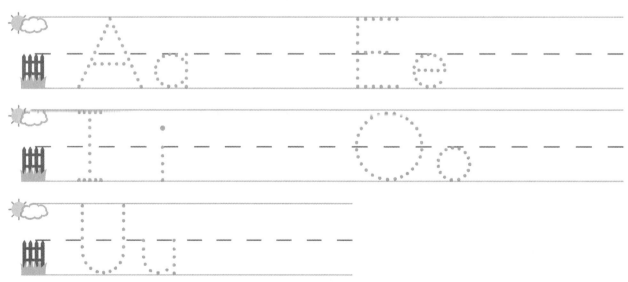

Aa  Ee

Ii  Oo

Uu

**Directions:** Name each picture. Color the pictures. Circle each vowel (*a, e, i, o, u*) in each word. Trace and write the vowels.

Name: _____

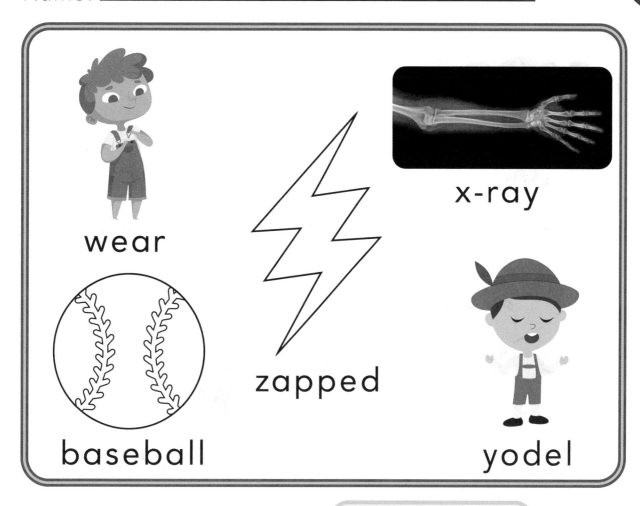

wear

baseball

zapped

x-ray

yodel

**Time to Draw**

**Directions:** Name each picture. Color the pictures. Circle the consonants *b*, *w*, *x*, *y*, and *z*. Draw your favorite word on this page.

**Letters and Sounds Review**

cheek

fly

high

goodies

daylight

## Time to Draw

**Directions:** Name each picture. Color the pictures. Circle the consonants *c, d, f, g,* and *h*. Draw yourself during the day.

# High-Frequency Words

## Let's Read Words in a Snap

In this section, students are introduced to 25 high-frequency words. These words are the most frequently written words in print. Educators may also call them "snap words," "sight words," "word-wall words," and so on. No matter what they are called or what list you use as a reference, the goal is for emergent readers to know these words immediately when they see them. To effectively learn these words, repetition is key. In this section, students will encounter one new word each day and explore that word.

## What You May Need

- jumbo pencils or short golf pencils
- crayons, colored pencils, or markers
- small, nonchoking objects for letter-covering activities (modeling clay, interlocking cubes, large coins, etc.)
- camera (*optional*)

## Understanding the Activities

Here are ways to support learning:

- Talk about writing each letter of the day accurately on the lines, using the language of "sky, fence, and grass" when writing the word of the day.
- If help is needed with fine-motor skills, adults may write letters with highlighters or light markers so students can trace the correct formation of each letter.
- Check out books available from your library to look for high-frequency words in print.
- You may wish to extend students' learning by making these words in other ways, such as using magnetic letters on a cookie tray, foam letters that stick to the sides of a bathtub, or alphabet blocks.
- You may wish to review the high-frequency words previously learned in this book: *a, an, at, am, go, no, so, be, he, me, we, in, is, it, I.*

up

High-Frequency Words

Name: _____

**Directions:** Trace the word *up* with your finger at least 5 times. Read the word. Use the word in a sentence. Cover the word with small objects. Color the pictures. Then, go on a scavenger hunt to find this word in print.

Name: _____

my          in

my

at          my

he

**my**

my          it

my          my

go          my

we

no          up

---

**Directions:** Trace the word *my* with your finger at least 5 times. Read the word. Touch and say each word. Find and circle each word *my*.

Name: _____

High-Frequency Words

| by | up | my | is |
|------|-------|-----|-------|
| blue | green | red | brown |

# The house is by the river.

**Directions:** Read the words. Use the key to color the picture. Read the sentence. Circle the word *by* in the sentence.

Name: _____

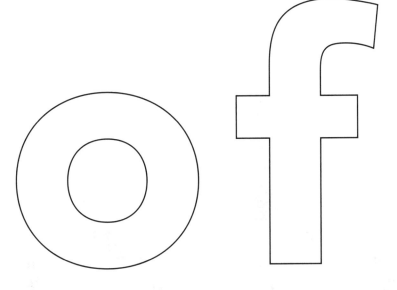

🧺 of 💐
basket    flowers

8

🥣 of 🍎
bowl    fruit

9

**Directions:** Trace the word *of* with your finger at least 5 times. Read the word. Color the letters. Use the word in a sentence. Then, circle the word *of* on the pages of the book.

Name: _____

**do**

High-Frequency Words

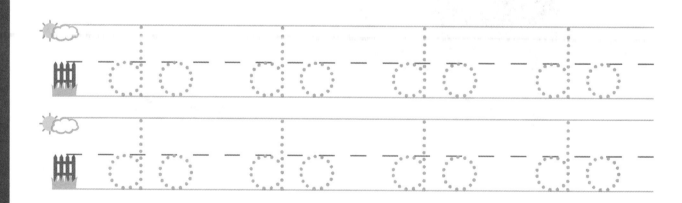

**Directions:** Trace around the word *do* with different colors. Read the word. Use the word in a sentence. Then, trace the words.

Name: _____

## Can you find **if**?

| a | i | f | b | i | f |
|---|---|---|---|---|---|
| d | g | q | h | x | j |
| i | f | s | i | f | w |
| k | m | u | t | z | a |
| y | i | f | v | n | r |
| p | y | g | w | i | f |

**Directions:** Read the word *if*. Then, find and circle the word 5 times in the word search.

Name:

on

High-Frequency Words

**Directions:** Trace the word *on* with your finger at least 5 times. Read the word. Use the word in a sentence. Cover the word with small objects. Color the pictures. Then, go on a scavenger hunt to find this word in print.

Name: _____

as     is

as

it

at     he

as     my     as

go     we     in

no     as     up

**Directions:** Trace the word *as* with your finger at least 5 times. Read the word. Use the word in a sentence. Find and circle each word *as*.

Name: _____

| to |
|---|

| to | on | as | go |
|---|---|---|---|
| blue | green | yellow | light brown |

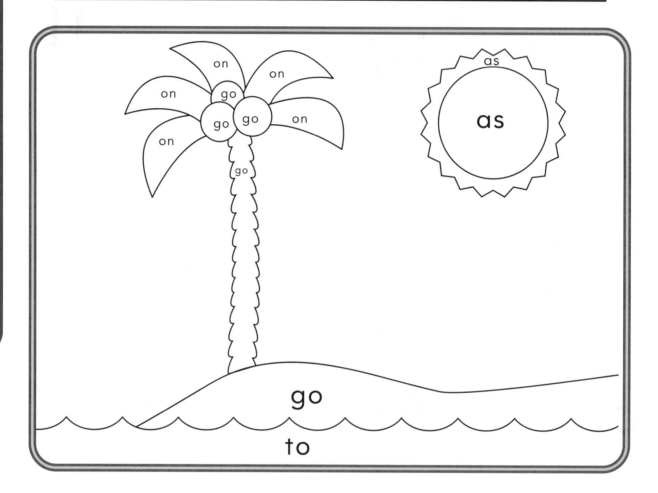

# I can go to the beach.

**Directions:** Read the words. Use the key to color the picture. Read the sentence. Circle the word *to* in the sentence.

© Shell Education

Name: _____

and

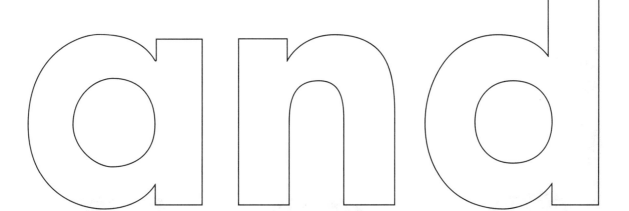

🌹 and 🌼

roses          daisies

**6**

🍎 and 🍊

apples          oranges

**8**

---

**Directions:** Trace the word *and* with your finger at least 5 times. Read the word. Color the letters. Use the word in a sentence. Then, circle the word *and* on the pages of the book.

Name: _____

her

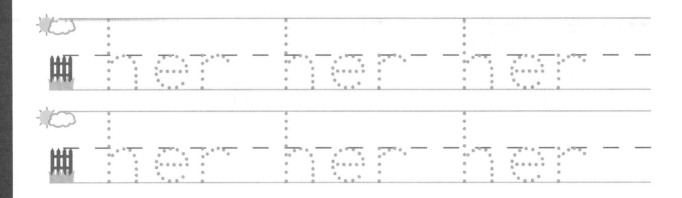

**Directions:** Trace around the word *her* with different colors. Read the word. Use the word in a sentence. Then, trace over the words.

High-Frequency Words

Name: ______________________

has

High-Frequency Words

Can you find **has**?

| | | | | | |
|---|---|---|---|---|---|
| a | i | f | h | a | s |
| h | a | s | n | x | j |
| i | f | h | a | s | w |
| k | h | u | t | z | a |
| y | i | h | a | s | r |
| h | a | s | w | i | f |

**Directions:** Read the word *has*. Then, find and circle the word 5 times in the word search.

see

Name: _____

**Directions:** Trace the word *see* with your finger at least 5 times. Read the word. Use the word in a sentence. Cover the word with small objects. Color the pictures. Then, go on a scavenger hunt to find this word in print.

she

she

by

he

at

my

she

as

she

in

go

of

up

no

she

she

**Directions:** Trace the word *she* with your finger at least 5 times. Read the word. Use the word in a sentence. Find and circle each word *she*.

are

Name: _____

High-Frequency Words

| the | in | are | see |
|-----|-----|-----|-----|
| black | green | yellow | red |

The birds are in the tree.

**Directions:** Read the words. Use the key to color the picture. Read the sentence. Circle the word *are* in the sentence.

Name: _____

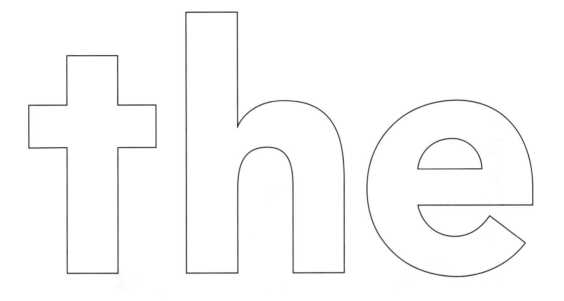

to the
store

2

at the
store

3

**Directions:** Trace the word *the* with your finger at least 5 times. Read the word. Color the letters. Use the word in a sentence. Then, circle the word *the* on the pages of the book.

Name: _____

**High-Frequency Words**

**his**

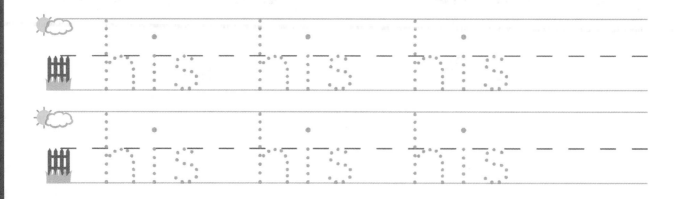

**Directions:** Trace around the word *his* with different colors. Read the word. Use the word in a sentence. Then, trace the words.

Name: _____

# Can you find **put**?

| a | p | u | t | c | s |
|---|---|---|---|---|---|
| h | a | x | p | u | t |
| i | p | u | t | v | w |
| k | j | u | a | s | b |
| p | u | t | u | z | r |
| o | a | v | p | u | t |

**Directions:** Read the word *put*. Then, find and circle the word 5 times in the word search.

get

Name: _____

**Directions:** Trace the word *get* with your finger at least 5 times. Read the word. Use the word in a sentence. Cover the word with small objects. Color the pictures. Then, go on a scavenger hunt to find this word in print.

Name: _____

she

was

to

at

he

by

as

was

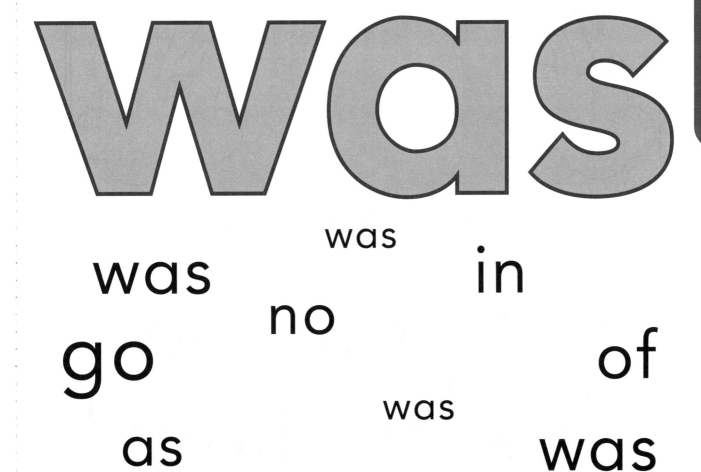

was

was

in

no

go

of

was

as

was

**Directions:** Trace the word *was* with your finger at least 5 times. Read the word. Use the word in a sentence. Find and circle each word *was*.

you

Name: _____

| to | it | see | do | you |
|----|----|-----|----|----|
| blue | green | yellow | orange | red |

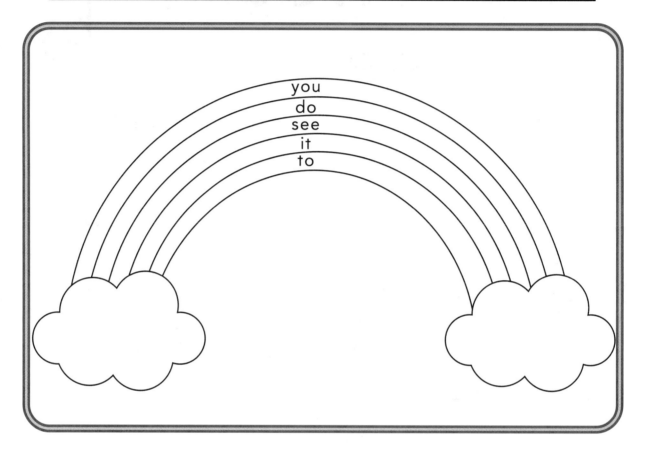

you
do
see
it
to

# Do you see the rainbow?

**Directions:** Read the words.  Use the key to color the picture.  Read the sentence.  Circle the word *you* in the sentence.

Name: _____

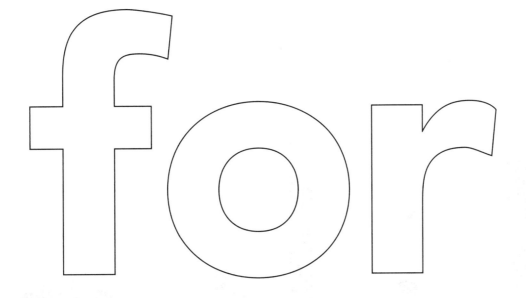

a  for you

truck

2

a  for you

cupcake

3

---

**Directions:** Trace the word *for* with your finger at least 5 times. Read the word. Color in the letters. Use the word in a sentence. Then, circle the word *for* on the pages of the book.

Name: _____

**like**

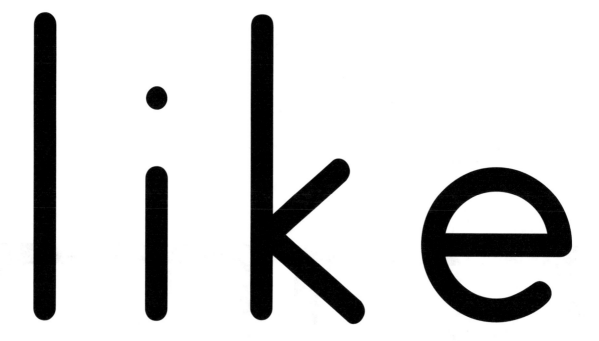

# like

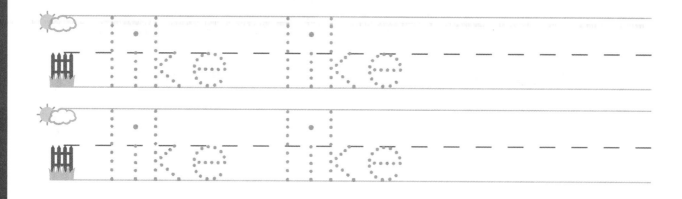

**Directions:** Trace around the word *like* with different colors. Read the word. Use the word in a sentence. Then, trace the words.

# Can you find **love**?

| z | i | l | o | v | e |
|---|---|---|---|---|---|
| h | b | s | n | o | j |
| l | o | v | e | s | w |
| k | l | o | v | e | a |
| y | i | h | e | s | r |
| l | o | v | e | i | l |

High-Frequency Words

**Directions:** Read the word *love.* Then, find and circle the word 4 times in the word search.

play

Name: _____

**Directions:** Trace the word *play* with your finger at least 5 times. Read the word. Use the word in a sentence. Cover the word with small objects. Color the pictures. Then, go on a scavenger hunt to find this word in print.

# Reading Simple Words

## Let's Blend Three-Letter Words

This will be an exciting section for students as they learn to blend three separate letter sounds together to read words. Word-family words are words that share a common pattern and are in the same "family." On the following pages, students will read three-letter word-family words. These words are also called consonant-vowel-consonant or CVC words. The words in this section have short vowel sounds as the middle letter in each word. Reading these words frequently with repetition will support learners to begin reading these words with automaticity.

## What You May Need

- jumbo pencils or short golf pencils
- crayons, colored pencils or markers
- camera (*optional*)

## Understanding the Activities

Here are ways to support learning:

- Watch for proper pencil grip.
- Read directions together, and invite students to go step-by-step.
- Have tools available, and set expectations for the workspace.
- Make sure students write the letters accurately.
- If help is needed with fine-motor skills, adults may write letters with highlighters or light markers so students can trace the correct formation of a letter.
- You may wish to extend students' learning by looking for these words in print and making them in other ways, such as using magnetic letters on a cookie tray, foam letters that stick to the sides of a bathtub, or alphabet blocks.

Reading Simple Words

Name: _____

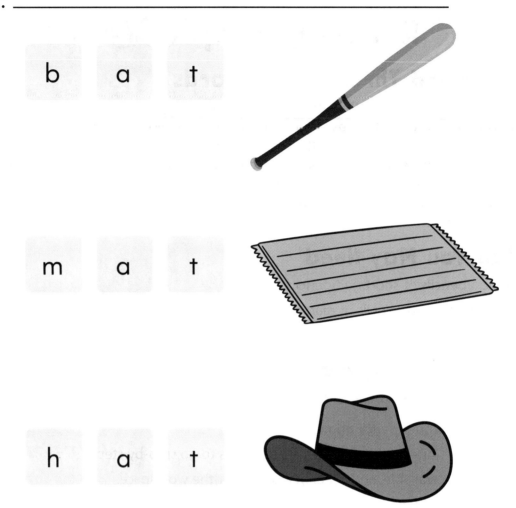

b a t

m a t

h a t

**Directions:** Tap on each letter with your finger. Say each sound. Read each word. Then, draw a picture to show one word that rhymes with these words.

Name: _____

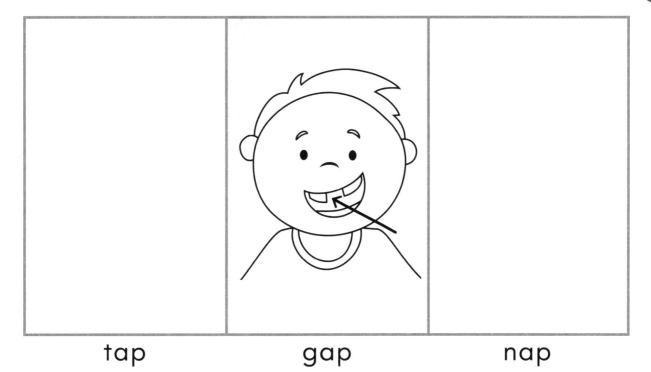

tap          gap          nap

mad          lad          sad

**Directions:** Read each word.  Color the pictures.  Draw a picture for each of the words without a picture.

Name: _____

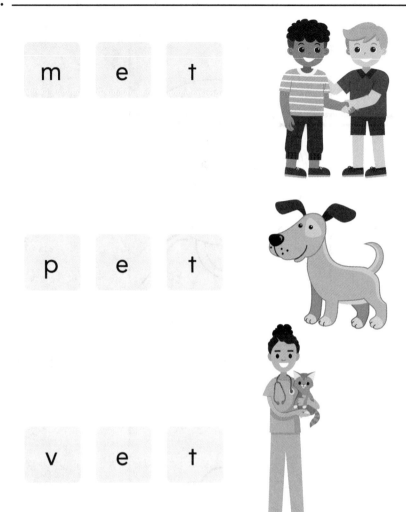

m  e  t

p  e  t

v  e  t

I met the pet at the vet.

**Directions:** Trace each letter in the words with your pointer finger. Say each sound. Read each word. Say words that rhyme with these words. Read the sentence. Then, draw a picture for it.

Name: ______________________



| | |
|---|---|
| get<br><br>pet | 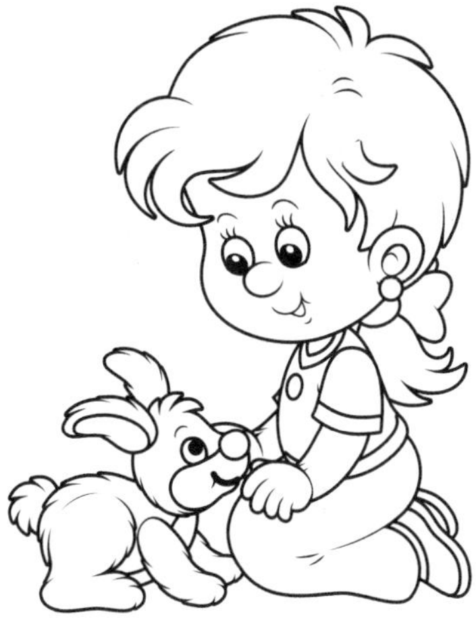 |
| met<br><br>jet | 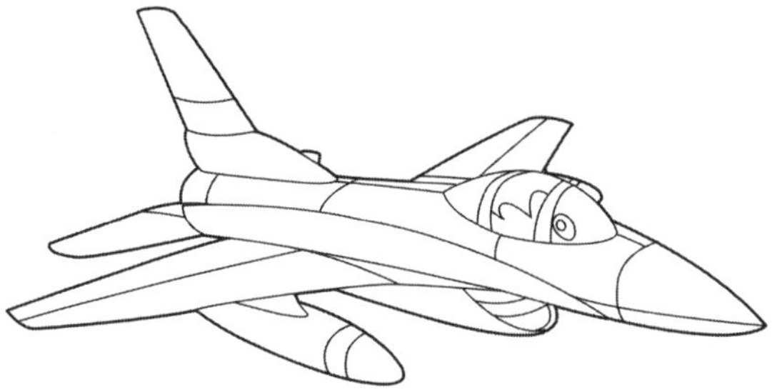 |
| hen<br><br>pen | 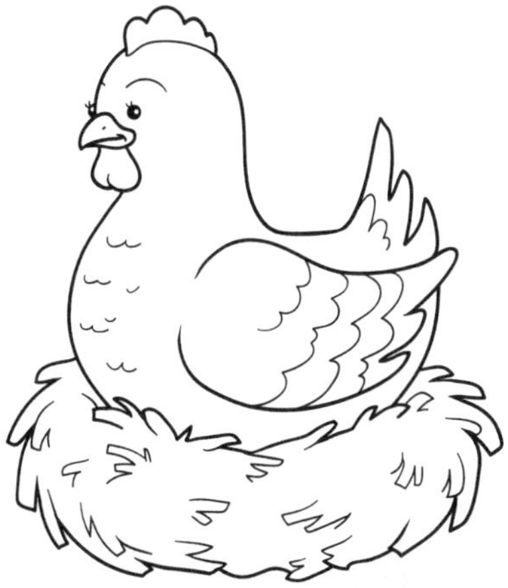 |

**Directions:** Read each word. Underline the vowel in each word (*e*). Circle the word that matches the picture. Color the pictures.

Name: _____

Reading Simple Words

k  i  t

l  i  t

s  i  t

---

**Directions:** Trace each letter in the words with your pointer finger. Say each sound. Read each word. Say words that rhyme with these words. Draw, color, and label a picture of one word that rhymes with these words.

---

Name: _____

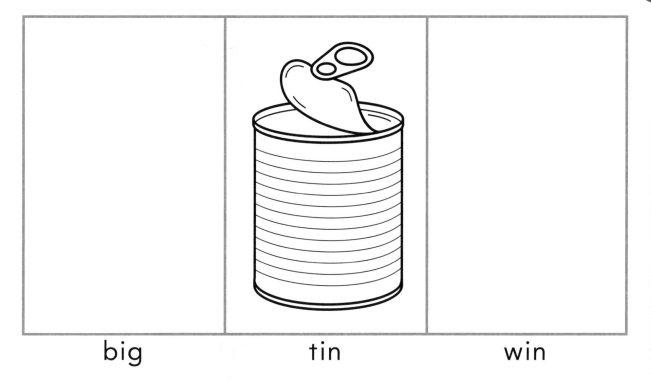

| big | tin | win |

| pig | hip | dig |

**Directions:** Read each word. Color the pictures. Draw a picture for each of the words without a picture.

Name: _____

Reading Simple Words

h    o    p

m    o    p

t    o    p

I can hop on top with a mop.

**Directions:** Trace each letter in the words with your pointer finger. Say each sound. Read each word. Say words that rhyme with these words. Read the sentence. Then, draw a picture for it.

Name: _____

ADY
160

Reading Simple Words

| bog / dog | |
| jog / cog | |
| log / fog | |
| dot / got | |

**Directions:** Read each word.  Underline the vowel in each word (*o*).  Circle the word that matches the picture.  Color the pictures.

© Shell Education

127442—180 Days of Reading for Prekindergarten

185

Name: _____

b  u  n

r  u  n

s  u  n

**Directions:** Trace each letter in the words with your pointer finger. Say each sound. Read each word. Say words that rhyme with these words. Draw, color, and label a picture of one word that rhymes with these words.

Name: _____

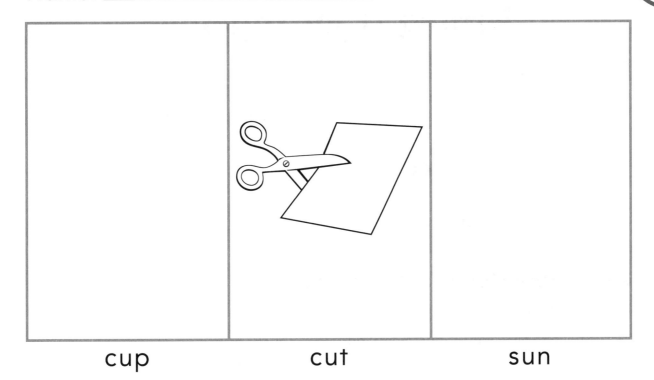

| cup | cut | sun |

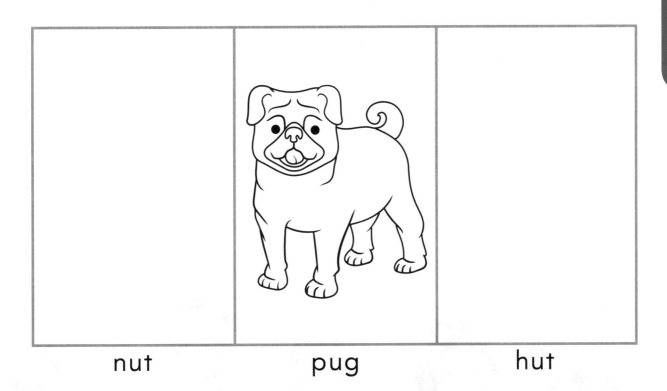

| nut | pug | hut |

**Directions:** Read each word. Color the pictures. Draw a picture for each of the words without a picture.

# Putting It All Together

## Let's Read!

In this final section, students put together all they have learned about alphabet letters and sounds, concepts of print, high-frequency words, and reading simple words. Students will confidently read the following pages to see themselves as readers.

## What You May Need

- jumbo pencils or short golf pencils
- crayons, colored pencils, or markers
- camera (*optional*)

## Understanding the Activities

Here are ways to support learning:

- Continue to encourage proper pencil grip.
- Read directions together, and invite students to go step-by-step.
- Have tools available, and set expectations for the workspace.
- You may wish to extend students' learning by reading books, magazines, applications, literature online, etc. Another extension might be to go to your school or local library to get a library card for future visits.

Name: _____

Scoops of
Loops

Scoops of yummy

**Directions:** Read each word aloud, with an adult. Track from left to right and top to bottom. Underline the word *of* in each sentence. Then, draw your favorite cereal.

Name: _____

I see a dolphin.

2

I see a seal.

3

**Directions:** Read each word aloud in the sentences, tracking from left to right.  Underline the word *see* in each sentence.  Draw where you might see these animals.

Name: _____

I look up to see the sun.

I look up to see the moon.

4

5

**Directions:** Read each word aloud in the sentences, tracking from left to right. Underline the word *up* in each sentence. Use your pointer finger in the air to "skywrite" the word *up* at least 5 times. Then, practice writing the word.

Name: _____

Putting It All Together

I like bread.

6

I like jelly.

7

**Directions:** Read each word aloud in the sentences, tracking from left to right. Circle the words *like* and *I* in each sentence. Draw other items that usually go together (like bread and jelly).

127442—180 Days of Reading for Prekindergarten

Name: _____

The *Zoom and Go* is the best toy car!

Watch the *Zoom and Go* race on by!

**Directions:** Read each word aloud with an adult, tracking from left to right. Circle the word *and* in each sentence and on the packaging. Draw your favorite toy.

**Putting It All Together**

Name: _____

I see her bat.

Do you see her mitt?

8

9

**Directions:** Read each word aloud in the sentences, tracking from left to right. Put a box around the word *her* in each sentence. Use your pointer finger in the air to "skywrite" the word *her* at least 5 times. Then, practice writing the word.

Name: _____

His hair is brown.

10

His shirt is brown.

11

**Directions:** Read each word aloud in the sentences, tracking from left to right. Put a box around the word *his* in each sentence. Draw yourself showing the color of your hair and shirt.

Name: _____

He put it in a bun.

Then, he was ready to eat.

12                                    13

**Directions:** Read each word aloud in the sentences, tracking from left to right. Put a box around the word *put* in each sentence. Use your pointer finger in the air to "skywrite" the word *put* at least 5 times. Then, practice writing the word.

Name: _____

## Come to *Papa's Pizza* for the best meal!

**Pizza for the whole family!**

We are here for your pizza needs.

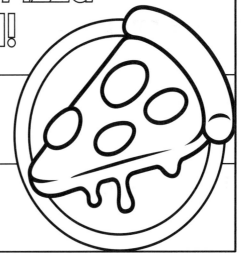

**Directions:** Read each word aloud with an adult, tracking from left to right. Put a box around the word *for* on the billboard. Draw your favorite pizza or food.

Name: _____

Putting It All Together

I see my pets.

I see my cat.

I see my dog.

**Directions:** Read each word in the sentences, tracking from left to right and top to bottom. Underline the word *see* in each sentence. Draw a pet.

Name: _____

I can jump rope.

I can jump up.

I can jump down.

I love to jump!

**Directions:** Read each word aloud in the sentences, tracking from left to right and top to bottom. Circle the word *jump* in each sentence. Jump and spell the word *jump* at least 5 times.

Name: _____

I love to eat!

I love to eat this.

I love to eat that.

**Directions:** Read each word in the sentences, tracking from left to right and top to bottom. Put a box around the word *love* in each sentence. Draw the food you love to eat.

Name: _____

## Candy that tastes *As Good as Gold*

**Directions:** Read each word aloud with an adult, tracking from left to right. Put a box around the word *as*. Draw your favorite candy.

Putting It All Together

He likes to
get toys!

He will get
a car.

He will get
a bear.

Do you like to get
toys too?

**Directions:** Read each word in the sentences, tracking from left to right and top to bottom. Return at the end of each line. Underline the word *get* in each sentence. Hop on one foot, and spell the word *get* at least 5 times.

Name: _____

Putting It All Together

She went to the
theme park.

She was by the
merry-go-round.

She was by
the swings.

**Directions:** Read each word in the sentences, tracking from left to right and top to bottom. Return at the end of each line. Put boxes around the words *she*, *was*, and *by*. Draw a theme park you might like to see.

Name: _____

We will go to the zoo.

We will see the monkey.

We will see the lion.

We like to go to the zoo!

**Directions:** Read each word in the sentences, tracking from left to right and top to bottom. Return at the end of each line. Put boxes around the words *we* and *to*. Clap your hands, and spell the word *we* and the word *to* at least 5 times.

Name: _____

# See what happens if you take a chance!

**Directions:** Read each word aloud with an adult, tracking from left to right and top to bottom. Put a box around each word *if*. Draw your favorite game to play.

# Congratulations!

## You did it!

### Congratulations to:

_____

### Achievement:

You worked hard for 180 days to learn how to read!

## Way to go!  You did your best!

**Awarded by:** _____      **Date:** _____

**Directions:** Read each word aloud with an adult, tracking from left to right and top to bottom.  Draw yourself as a reader.  Post this certificate somewhere special.

# Answer Key

## pages 69–73, 120–123

Here are some sample words that students can use in their drawings:

Long *a*: ape, acorn
Short *a*: astronaut, apple, ant
Long *e*: easel, eel, eagle
Short *e*: egg, elephant, exercise
Long *i*: icicle, ice cream, island
Short *i*: igloo, insect, instruments, iguana
Long *o*: ocean, oatmeal, oval, overalls
Short *o*: otter, octopus, ox
Long *u*: uniform, utensils
Short *u*: umpire, up, unhappy

## page 153

## page 154

## page 157

| a | i | f | b | i | f |
|---|---|---|---|---|---|
| d | g | q | h | x | j |
| i | f | s | i | f | w |
| k | m | u | t | z | a |
| y | i | f | v | n | r |
| p | y | g | w | i | f |

## page 159

## page 160

## page 163

| a | i | f | h | a | s |
|---|---|---|---|---|---|
| h | a | s | n | x | j |
| i | f | h | a | s | w |
| k | h | u | t | z | a |
| y | i | h | a | s | r |
| h | a | s | w | i | f |

## page 165

# Answer Key *(cont.)*

**page 166**

**page 169**

| a | p | u | t | c | s |
|---|---|---|---|---|---|
| h | a | x | p | u | t |
| i | p | u | t | v | w |
| k | j | u | a | s | b |
| p | u | t | u | z | r |
| o | a | v | p | u | t |

**page 171**

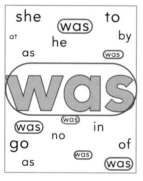

**page 172**

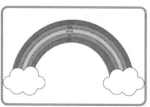

**page 175**

| z | i | l | o | v | e |
|---|---|---|---|---|---|
| h | h | s | n | o | j |
| l | o | v | e | s | w |
| k | l | o | v | e | a |
| y | i | h | e | s | r |
| l | o | v | e | i | l |

**page 181**

Students should circle pet, jet, and hen.

**page 185**

Students should circle dog, jog, log, and dot.

# The Alphabet

**Directions:** Use your finger to trace each letter as you say its name.

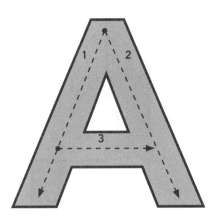
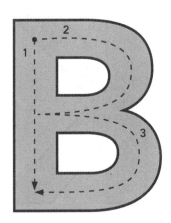
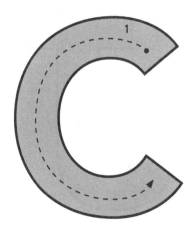

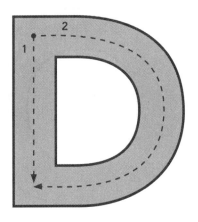
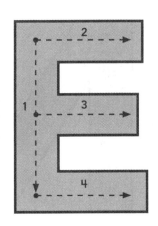
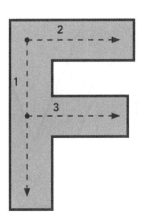

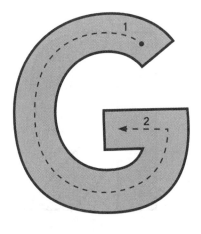
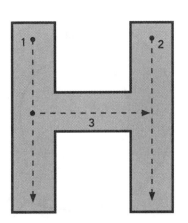
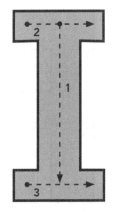

# The Alphabet

**Directions:** Use your finger to trace each letter as you say its name.

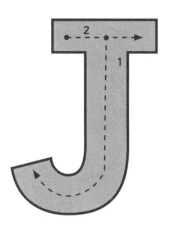 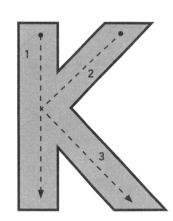 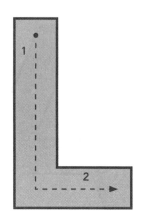

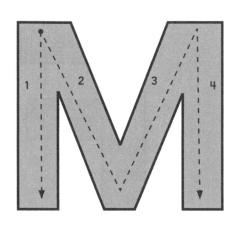 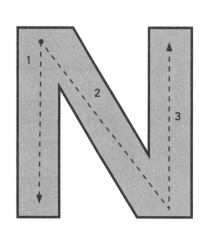 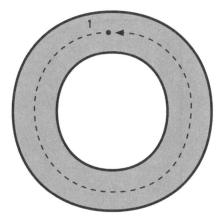

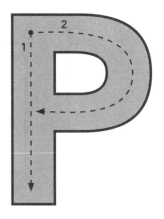 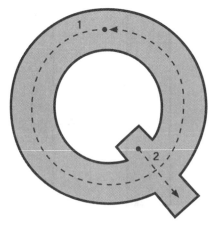 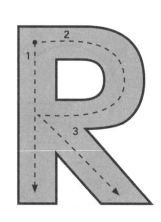

# The Alphabet

**Directions:** Use your finger to trace each letter as you say its name.

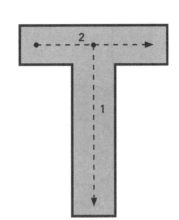
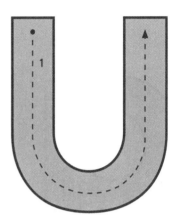

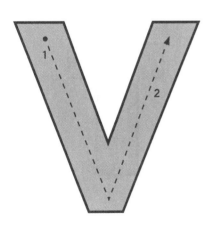
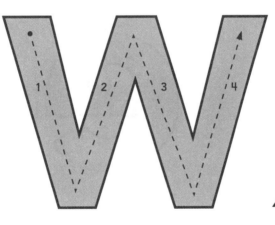
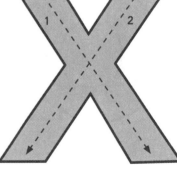

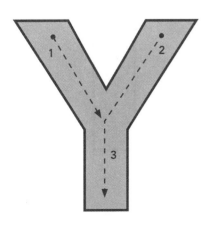
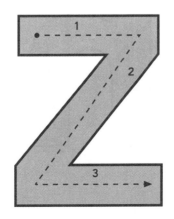

# The Alphabet

**Directions:** Use your finger to trace each letter as you say its name.

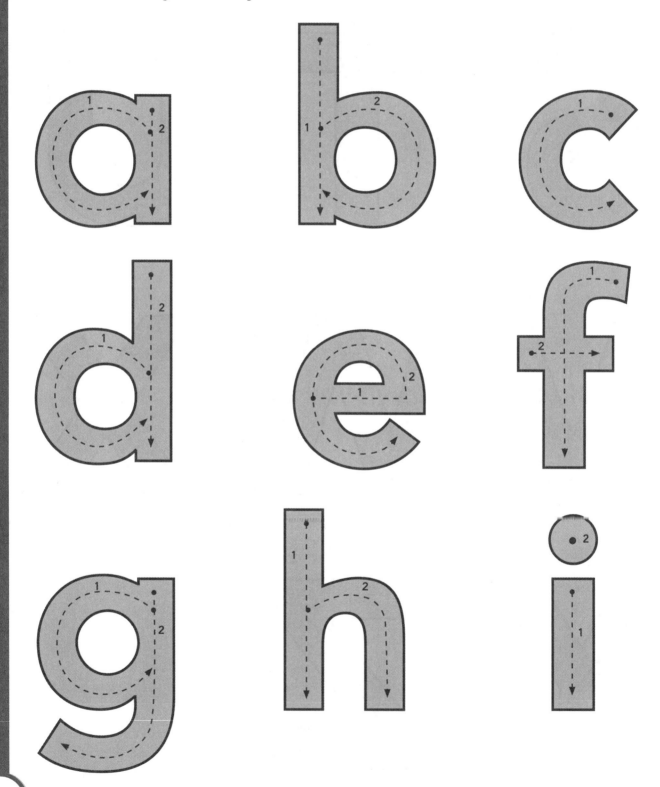

# The Alphabet

**Directions:** Use your finger to trace each letter as you say its name.

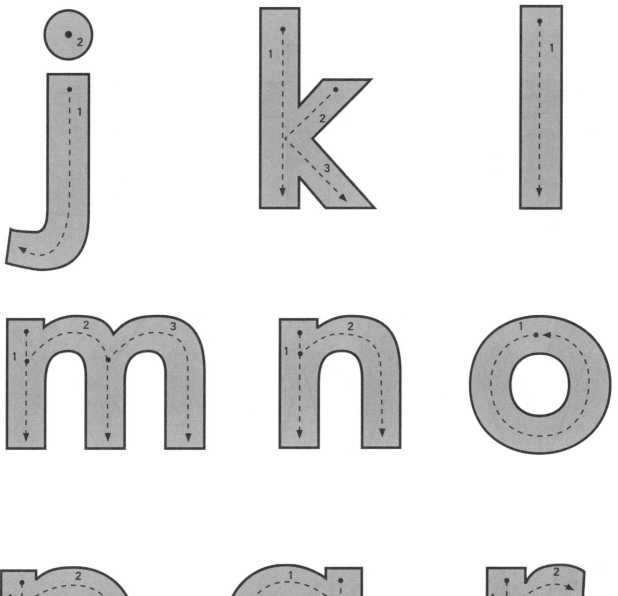

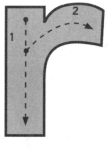

# The Alphabet

**Directions:** Use your finger to trace each letter as you say its name.

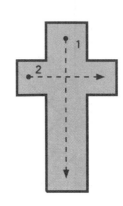
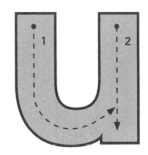

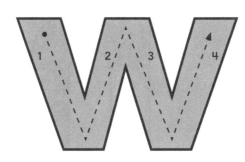

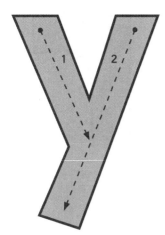
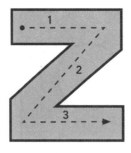

# References Cited

California Department of Education. 2012. *The Alignment of the California Preschool Learning Foundations with Key Early Education Resources.* Sacramento: California Department of Education.

First Things First. 2017. "Early Childhood Brain Development Has Lifelong Impact." *Arizona PBS.* azpbs.org/2017/11/early-childhood-brain-development-lifelong-impact.

Fry, Edward. 1999. *1,000 Instant Words: The Most Common Words for Teaching Reading, Writing, and Spelling.* Garden Grove, CA: Teacher Created Resources.

Hirsch, Megan. 2010. *How to Hold a Pencil.* Los Angeles, CA: Hirsch Indie Press.

Olsen, Jan Z. 2018. *Letters and Numbers for Me Teacher's Guide: Kindergarten.* Gaithersburg, MD: Handwriting Without Tears.

National Reading Panel. 2000. *Teaching Children to Read: An Evidence-Based Assessment of the Scientific Research Literature on Reading and Its Implication for Reading Instruction.* (NIH Publication No. 00-4769). Washington, DC: U.S. Government Printing Office. www.nichd.nih.gov/sites/default/files/publications/pubs/nrp/Documents/report.pdf.

# Suggested Websites

| Website Title | Address | Content |
| --- | --- | --- |
| ABC Mouse | www.abcmouse.com | alphabet, phonics |
| Learning A–Z | www.learninga-z.com | alphabet, phonics |
| Starfall | www.starfall.com | alphabet, phonics, emergent reading |
| Epic! | www.getepic.com | reading books and videos |
| Raz-Kids | www.raz-kids.com | books for emergent readers (subscription) |
| National Geographic Kids | www.kids.nationalgeographic.com | reading books (subscription) |
| Storybots | storybots.com | songs with videos for A-to-Z letters |

# Digital Resources

## Accessing the Digital Resources

The digital resources can be downloaded by following these steps:

1. Go to **www.tcmpub.com/digital**

2. Use the ISBN number to redeem the digital resources.

3. Respond to the question using the book.

4. Follow the prompts on the Content Cloud website to sign in or create a new account.

5. Choose the digital resources you would like to download. You can download all the files at once, or a specific group of files.

   - **Please note:** Some files provided for download have large file sizes. Download times for these larger files vary based on your download speed.

**ISBN:**
**9781087652023**

## Contents of the Digital Resources

### Activities

- Ideas for extending the learning to real-world situations
- Templates for creating word pattern books
- Hands-on practice for learning uppercase and lowercase letters
- Writing practice of uppercase and lowercase letters

### Teacher Resources

- Introducing the Concept pages
- Certificate of Completion
- Standards Correlation